# THE
# BURTON HISTORICAL COLLECTION

*Clarence Monroe Burton*

A
# Genealogical Guide
to the
# BURTON
# HISTORICAL
# COLLECTION
Detroit Public Library

JOSEPH F. OLDENBURG

P.O. Box 476
Salt Lake City, UT 84110

*ISBN 0-916489-33-7*

*First Printing 1988*
*10 9 8 7 6 5 4 3 2*

*Library of Congress Cataloging-in-Publication Data*
*Oldenburg, Joseph F., 1944-*
*A genealogical guide to the Burton Historical Collection.*
*Bibliography: p.*
*Includes index.*
*1. United States--Genealogy--Bibliography--Catalogs.*
*2. United States--History, Local--Bibliography--Catalogs.*
*3. Genealogy--Bibliography--Catalogs.*
*4.Burton Historical Collection--Catalogs.*
*5. Detroit Public Library--Catalogs.*
*I. Burton Historical Collection. II. Title.*
*Z5313.U5054 1988 [CS47] 016.929'373 88-7560*
*ISBN 0-916489-33-7*

*Printed in the United States of America*

To my wife, Carol,
my daughter, Gretchen, and
my late daughter, Robin

# Contents

Immigration and Naturalization Records
Military Records
Vital Records
City Directories
Patriotic and Hereditary Societies
Surnames
Maps and Atlases
Land Records
Newspapers
Ethnic Groups
Black Genealogy
Heraldry and Nobility
Coats of Arms
Miscellaneous

*New England and Eastern States*
Maine
New Hampshire
Vermont
Massachusetts
Rhode Island
Connecticut
New York
Pennsylvania
New Jersey
Delaware
Maryland
District of Columbia
*Southern States*
West Virginia
Virginia
North Carolina
South Carolina
Georgia
Florida
Alabama
Mississippi
Louisiana
Texas
Arkansas

# Acknowledgements

A work of this type could not be successfully completed without the help and support of several people. I would like to thank the following: Robert Welsh of Ancestry Incorporated for his support and patience throughout the preparation of the manuscript of this work; Donna Valley Russell for the reading of the typescript and for insightful, helpful suggestions concerning changes and additions; Shirlie Moloney Huber for her dedication and for her excellent typing of the final version; and my wife, Carol, for typing a portion of the initial manuscript and for her love and support throughout the researching and writing of this book.

# Illustrations

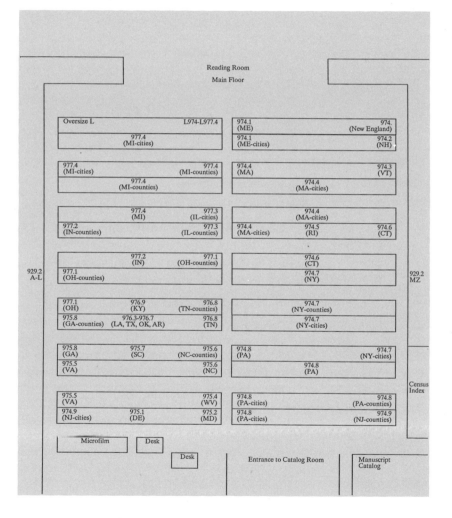

Plan of the Reading Room Main Floor

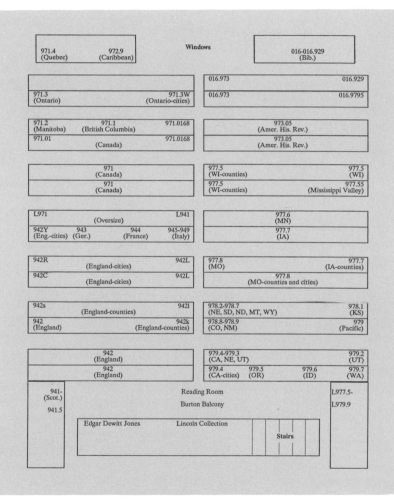

| | | | |
|---|---|---|---|
| 971.4 (Quebec) | 972.9 (Caribbean) | **Windows** | 016-016.929 (Bib.) |

| | | | |
|---|---|---|---|
| | | 016.973 | 016.929 |
| 971.3 (Ontario) | 971.3W (Ontario-cities) | 016.973 | 016.9795 |

| | | |
|---|---|---|
| 971.2 (Manitoba) | 971.1 (British Columbia) | 971.0168 |
| 971.01 | (Canada) | 971.0168 |

973.05 (Amer. His. Rev.)
973.05 (Amer. His. Rev.)

971 (Canada)
971 (Canada)

977.5 (WI-counties) — 977.5 (WI)
977.5 (WI-counties) — 977.55 (Mississippi Valley)

L971 (Oversize) L941
942Y (Eng.-cities) 943 (Ger.) 944 (France) 945-949 (Italy)

977.6 (MN)
977.7 (IA)

942R (England-cities) 942L
942C (England-cities) 942L

977.8 (MO) — 977.7 (IA-counties)
977.8 (MO-counties and cities)

942s (England-counties) 942I
942 (England) 942k (England-counties)

978.2-978.7 (NE, SD, ND, MT, WY) — 978.1 (KS)
978.8-978.9 (CO, NM) — 979 (Pacific)

942 (England)
942 (England)

979.4-979.3 (CA, NE, UT) — 979.2 (UT)
979.4 (CA-cities) 979.5 (OR) 979.6 (ID) 979.7 (WA)

941- (Scot.)
941.5

Reading Room
Burton Balcony

Edgar Dewitt Jones    Lincoln Collection

**Stairs**

L977.5-
L979.9

## Plan of the Reading Room Balcony

# Foreword

My introduction to the Burton Historical Collection, which occupies part of the north wing of the Detroit Public Library, occurred in 1970. Since then, my life has not been the same. For the next twelve years, I would be waiting impatiently for the doors to be unlocked every Saturday morning and then working until the warning bell sounded at the end of the day. Until 1977, as Chairman (and sole member) of the Research Committee of the Detroit Society for Genealogical Research, I answered yearly about 350 requests for genealogical assistance addressed to the Burton Historical Collection and the genealogical society. This was one of the most valuable experiences a fledgling genealogist could have. Searching for answers led me into most areas of the library. Questions related to wide geographical areas, often beyond Michigan, and frequently the fascinating and well-catalogued private papers and manuscript collection were explored. Joe Oldenburg, as Curator of Manuscripts for many of those years, was a knowledgeable, helpful, and enthusiastic guide. I was probably a pest, but he never failed to find answers to my frequent questions.

A two- or three-day visit to the Burton Hisorical Collection cannot begin to acquaint the newcomer with the vast resources of the collection. This long-needed guide is, therefore, essential. Joe Oldenburg, now Assistant Director of the Detroit Public Library, is uniquely well-qualified to author this guide, which describes the collection in both geographical area and subject, pointing out areas of particular strength or weakness and suggesting major sources for research in all the American states and certain Canadian provinces. It will prove invaluable for planning your research in any large genealogical library. By so doing, you may avoid the answer I heard so often, "Have you checked the card catalogue?"

*Donna Valley Russell*
Certified Genealogist,
Fellow, American Society of Genealogists

# *Introduction*

For many years, the Burton Historical Collection has been one of the best genealogical collections in the United States. Unfortunately, its unique system of numbering titles, along with other factors, have made it difficult for patrons to use. It is hoped that this book will remedy that situation so that all genealogists may appreciate this wonderful research collection and find it easier to use.

There are some things readers should keep in mind while reading this book. The Burton Historical Collection is a department within the Detroit Public Library. It is located on the first floor of the North Wing of the Main Library, and the address is 5201 Woodward Avenue, Detroit, Michigan. The Collection and all its materials are open to the public. The hours of the Main Library are the same as those of the Burton Collection: 9:30 A.M.-5:30 P.M. Monday, Tuesday, Thursday, Friday, Saturday; and Wednesday 9:00 A.M.-9:00 P.M. It is closed Sunday.

The Burton Collection is a reference collection; therefore, everything must be used in the Reading Room, and none of the materials may be checked out. The photocopying of materials by patrons is prohibited, and requests by mail are not accepted; however, photocopies will be made for patrons who visit the Burton Collection. Payment must be made when the order is placed. It should be borne in mind that a period of ten to fourteen days will elapse before the copies are ready. They will be mailed to the person concerned, if requested, or they may be collected.

The staff of the Burton Collection does not answer genealogical queries by mail; rather, a list of qualified genealogists who undertake research for a fee is sent in an attempt to deal with many inquiries and to best assist the public.

# 1
## *History of the Burton Collection*

The Burton Historical Collection was begun as the private collection of Clarence Monroe Burton, an attorney and collector of local history. Clarence Burton's life had about it the drama of the old West and the perseverance of a Horatio Alger. His father, Charles Burton, was a doctor in Battle Creek, Michigan. In 1848 when gold was discovered at Sutter's Mill, the good doctor was struck with gold fever. Taking his wife, Ann, and young son, Charles, he went to seek his fortune in the gold fields of California. Dr. Burton soon found that he could not support his young family on the little gold he found; so, within the mining community, he began to practice medicine again.

While the Burton family was living in Whiskey Diggings, one of the many mining towns that quickly grew up, Clarence Monroe Burton was born on 18 November 1853. Dr. Burton was away tending to an illness when Ann Burton gave birth, with the help of an old miner named Joe Stender. Soon after Clarence's birth, Dr. Burton realized that his dream of striking it rich would never be brought to fruition; therefore, he decided to return to Michigan and the full-time practice of medicine. His adventures did not end in California. He and his family boarded a ship out of San Francisco to return to the East around South America. Not long after they set sail, a band of pirates overtook the ship, relieved everyone of their gold, and sank the vessel. Not everyone lost their gold, however. Anticipating just such an event, Dr. Burton took a large nugget and sewed it into the hem of his wife's dress. In later years, Clarence would tell the story of his mother swimming to shore from the sinking ship, struggling to hold up her young son while being pulled down by the weight of the gold in her skirt.

The Burton family eventually reached Michigan in 1855, and Dr. Burton set up a practice in Hastings, Michigan. Young Clarence attended the public schools in Hastings, and, in 1869 attended the University of Michigan at Ann Arbor. He began his studies in literature but eventually changed to law. He graduated as an attorney in 1874. In that year, a judge from Detroit, Charles T. Walker, came to the law school to give a lecture entitled "The Northwest in the Revolution." During the lecture, the judge said, while holding up a leaf from an account book of 1780, "I think it is well for every professional man to have a hobby outside of his regular vocation. To this hobby, he should give as much of his time as is possible, together with his close thought and enthusiasm." In later years, Clarence Burton told this story to explain why he had collected the large group of materials that comprised his private library. He claimed that the lecture and the old account book gave him the idea that, being a book lover, he would collect a book on American history each day.

After his graduation from the University of Michigan, Mr. Burton, who already had a wife and the first of several children, went to Detroit seeking employment. He found a position in the law firm of John Ward and Eugene Skinner, who were engaged in title searching and making abstracts of land titles. Because the volume of land sales in Detroit had grown so, the searching of each title through the land records to establish ownership was becoming too time-consuming. Ward and Skinner decided to set up a "plant"; that is, to compile for each parcel of land a history that could be used for future title abstracts. To accumulate the information for these abstracts, they put their newest employee, Clarence Burton, to the task of combing through family histories, records of birth and death, marriages, wills, cemetery records, land records, and other sources. Clarence had a penchant for thoroughness and exactness, and he thrived on this type of work. It is obvious that Mr. Burton's involvement in the abstract and title business was the inspiration that led him to his consuming interest in local history. The necessity of collecting not only local, city, and county records but newspapers and personal records of all kinds, brought him into contact with much of the early history of the region. It is no wonder that he grew conversant in Detroit's history and, perhaps more than any other man, he came to appreciate its origins.

In 1883, Clarence Burton was made a partner in the firm. By that time, Eugene Skinner had left the firm to pursue a career in medicine. In 1891, Mr. Burton bought out John Ward's interest in the firm and organized the Burton Abstract and Title Company.

Mr. Burton was an indefatigable collector. He would root through people's attics and basements. Once he took his wagon out on a Sunday and emptied an outhouse full of the papers of William Woodbridge, who had been Michigan's first delegate to Congress, governor, and United

1 The Residence of Clarence M. Burton, 27 Brainard Street, Detroit, *ca.* 1891.
*Detroit Illustrated, 1891*

States Senator. In 1905, Mr. Burton was called to Ecorse to the home of the recently deceased Judge Halmer H. Emmons. Judge Emmons's papers were strewn over the floor of the home. With a pitchfork, Burton scooped them into seven barrels and took his treasure back to Detroit. In that pile of papers, he found the *Pontiac Journal,* an account of the siege of Detroit in 1763 by the Ottawa Indians, led by their Chief, Pontiac. The journal had been known to exist in the 1840s but had then disappeared. If Mr. Burton's reputation as a collector had not gone before him, the journal would have been lost forever.

By 1914 Clarence Burton's private library had become substantial to the extent that it took up a large part of his home at 27 Brainard Street. He had purchased land to build a new house on Boston Boulevard and made plans to donate his private collection to the Detroit Public Library. He deeded his collection to the library with two stipulations: the first being that a fireproof place should be provided in the newly

2 The Detroit Public Library, Main Library, in which the Burton
Historical Collection is housed. Cass Avenue facade.

planned city library (this being the Main Library today); the second that
the name Burton should be somehow associated with the collection.
The former Burton residence at 27 Brainard was included in the gift. On
25 September 1915, the house, now remodeled and equipped for library
service, was opened to the public as the Burton Historical Collection.
When the new Detroit Main Library was opened in June 1921, Mr. Burton suggested that the Library Commission convey back to him the
house on Brainard Street, and, in return, he would establish a $50,000
endowment for the future purchase of materials for the collection.

Judicious investment has vastly increased the size of the original
Burton Endowment Fund. Today the interest from the fund is used to
purchase additional material for the collection.

# 2
# *Card Catalogs and Floor Plans*

## Burton Card Catalog Room

The first room a visitor enters in the Burton Collection is the Card Catalog Room. There are a total of fifteen card catalogs around the walls of this room. Some are general and cover all subjects in the collection while others are very specific and deal only with certain subjects, such as local history or genealogy. Each catalog will be discussed in detail.

The floor plan of the Card Catalog Room (see figure 4) depicts the arrangement of the catalogs. Though the catalogs have been numbered on the floor plan, the visitor will not find numbers similar to these on the catalogs themselves. The numbers are used on this plan and in this book simply as a means to differentiate the catalogs for the understanding of the reader. As for the titles, the catalogs actually carry the words that are printed on the floor plan. For example, No. 5, Atlases and Maps, reads "Atlases" or "Maps" on a card on each drawer of that catalog. And, No.12, Vital Records, reads "Vital Records" on a card on each drawer of that particular catalog.

### Burton Main Catalog (No. 1 on the Floor Plan)

This is the main card catalog of the Burton Historical Collection. It is a dictionary catalog, which means that there is a card for each book filed under the name of the book's author, title, and the subjects covered therein. All of the cards are interfiled alphabetically in the card catalog. The catalog contains all the different types of printed material in the Burton Collection such as books, magazines, broadsides, newspapers, pamphlets, atlases, abstracts, and newspaper clipping files.

The subjects in this catalog cover virtually the entire range of subjects in the Burton Collection, one of the most important of which is

3 The Burton Historical Collection Reading Room, *ca.* 1972,
and basically the same today.
*D'Arcy, MacManus, Intermatco, Inc.*

individual family histories. For example, if the researcher were looking for a history of the Armstrong family, he would look under the words "Armstrong family." Listed there would be volumes devoted to the subject or books that contain material which relates to the Armstrong family. Or, if the researcher were trying to determine whether Burton had individual histories on the Lincoln family, he would look under the words "Lincoln family." On the cards would be listed all titles on that family or books dealing with other families and subjects that refer to the Lincolns.

Histories of cities, counties, states, and Canadian provinces are also found in the Burton Collection main card catalog. The researcher would look for these under the name of the locality. For example, to determine which histories the Burton Collection holds for Rutland, Vermont, he would look under RUTLAND, VT.–HISTORY. Books dealing with the history of the city will be found under that subject heading. For a county history, the listing would be found under the name of the county and state, for example, WAYNE COUNTY, MICH.–HISTORY. A state would be listed under its name; the Canadian provinces listed under their names:

Picture of Pontiac's Conspiracy

The Burton Catalog

1. **Burton Main Catalog** (white card)
   family history, countries, states, counties, cities, Canadian provinces, magazines, newspapers

2. **Check List** (pink)
   dates of magazines and newspapers in Burton

3. **Local History** (orange)
   Michigan and Detroit history

4. **Great Lakes History** (blue)
   history of ships and shipwrecks on the Great Lakes

5. **Atlases and Maps** (pink)

6. **Pictures** (white)
   Michigan and Detroit Pictures by Subject

7. **Detroit Chronology** (white)
   events in Detroit history

8. **Wayne County Coroners Files**
   Coroners reports of deaths in Wayne County, Michigan, 1870-88

9. **Newspaper Chronology**
   Detroit and Michigan newspapers held by Burton, 1809-73

10. **Genealogical Index**
    family history

11. **Coats of Arms** (white)

12. **Vital Records** (green)
    census, birth, death, marriage, tax lists

13. **Military Service Lists** (white)
    from Colonial Wars through War of 1898

14. **DSGR Charts** (orange)
    genealogy charts of members of Detroit Society for Genealogical Research

15. **Detroit and Michigan Biography Index** (blue)
    Detroit and Michigan people

Entrance to
Reading Room

| | |
|---|---|
| 9 | |
| 8 | |
| 7 | |
| 6 | |
| 5 | |
| 4 | |
| 3 | 10 |
| 2 | 11 |
| | 12 |
| 1 | 13 |
| | 14 |
| | 15 |

4  Plan of the Card Catalog Room,
the Burton Historical Collection

for example, MICHIGAN-HISTORY, ONTARIO-HISTORY, or QUEBEC-HISTORY.

All the newspapers and magazines in the Burton Collection are listed in the main card catalog. They are listed by name and the subjects covered therein. For example, *The American Genealogist,* the *Detroit Society for Genealogical Research Magazine, The Genealogical Helper,* and *Tree Talks* would all be listed under the exact name of the magazine. Newspapers such as the *Ann Arbor News,* the *Detroit Free Press,* the *Michigan Volksblatt,* and the *Pontiac Gazette* are listed under their exact names. The magazines listed above would also be listed under the subject GENEALOGY-PERIODICALS. The newspapers would be found under NEWSPAPERS-ANN ARBOR or the city of publication.

Frequently, when one locates a magazine or newspaper, the words "For number of volumes in library see Check List" will be stamped in the middle of the card. At this point the researcher would go to the Check List (No. 2).

### Check List (No. 2)

This catalog records the years and issues of a magazine or newspaper held by the Burton Collection. For example, the catalog lists exactly which issues Burton has of *The American Genealogist,* the *Detroit Free Press,* or any other magazine or newspaper.

There is a separate set of drawers labeled the "Newspaper Check List." This contains only bound volumes of newspapers held in the collection. If only loose issues of a newspaper are held, the card will read "See Newspaper Sheet Records" (a complete list of all bound newspapers and loose issues). It is kept in the staff workroom, and the researcher must request it at the Reference Desk in the Reading Room.

The Newspaper Check List for the *Detroit Free Press* would indicate that Burton holds the years 1831-1959. The issues of the *Detroit Free Press* since 1959 are on microfilm in the General Information Department of the Detroit Main Library.

### Local History (No. 3)

The local history catalog contains information on geographical areas in the United States and Canada. The first two drawers deal with Canada and states other than Michigan. The remainder of the drawers cover the cities and counties of Michigan. There is one section dedicated entirely to Detroit.

This catalog includes articles from newspapers, magazines, and books arranged by subject under state and city name, for example, MINNESOTA-SCHOOLS or MICHIGAN-HOTELS or MICHIGAN-LOCALITIES-

DEARBORN. The Detroit section occupies more than half this catalog and is a comprehensive arrangement of subjects on virtually every aspect of the city's history. The same classification by localities and subject matter is used. A full range of subjects cannot be listed here but the following few examples will suffice: churches, fires, hotels, industries, and business houses, monuments, organizations, schools, streets, street cars, time, and zoos.

A researcher looking for information on churches in Detroit would look under DETROIT-CHURCHES, then under the denomination and name of the church. An example would be DETROIT-CHURCHES-LUTHERAN-RIVERSIDE. This entry would relate to articles on the Riverside Lutheran Church in Detroit.

A search for information on a particular street in Detroit would be another example. First, one would look under the heading DETROIT-STREETS, then the name of the street. The heading DETROIT-STREETS-WOODWARD would refer to an article on Woodward Avenue in Detroit.

### Great Lakes History (No. 4)

The history of the Great Lakes is intertwined with the history of the Midwest and especially with Detroit and Michigan. This catalog lists articles in newspapers, magazines, and books having to do with shipping and life on the Great Lakes. The first two drawers contain entries on such material as disasters, fisheries, islands, lighthouses, shipbuilding, steamship lines, and storms.

The majority of the file is an alphabetical list of articles on ships that have sailed the Great Lakes. The articles may describe the construction of a ship, its travels on the Lakes, or, more frequently, its sinking.

### Atlases and Maps (No. 5)

This is actually several catalogs. The first includes the atlases and is found in only two drawers. One drawer lists atlases by date and the other by locality. For example, the *Belden Atlas Of Wayne County, Michigan* is listed in the first catalog under 1876, the year of publication. In the second catalog it is listed alphabetically by locality, WAYNE COUNTY-MICHIGAN.

The map catalog is actually four different catalogs. In the first, the maps are arranged alphabetically under the cartographer's name; the second catalog lists the maps by date; in the third, each is arranged by locality; and the last is organized by type of map, such as electoral or topographical.

For example, a Detroit map of 1853 by Henry Hart, which includes the voting wards of the city, would be filed in the first catalog under the cartographer, HART, HENRY. In the second catalog, it would be listed under 1853. In the third catalog, the map would be filed under Detroit. In the last catalog, the map would be filed under ELECTORAL MAPS–DETROIT.

## Pictures (No. 6)

This catalog, strongest in the area of the Great Lakes, Michigan, and Detroit, contains listings of the drawings, prints, lithographs, negatives, photographs, and pictures from books. The arrangement is by locality, then subject. The same localities and subjects used in the Local History Catalog (No. 3) are used in this catalog. For example, if searching for a picture of Central High School in Detroit, one would look under DETROIT–SCHOOLS–CENTRAL. If researching pictures of Woodward Avenue, one would look under DETROIT–STREETS–WOODWARD.

The Great Lakes pictures are predominantly composed of illustrations of ships. For example, there are artists' renderings of the *Griffon,* the first European ship to sail on the Great Lakes (1679), and the *Walk-in-the-Water,* the first steamship to sail on the Great Lakes (1818). There are photographs of the thousands of steam and sailing ships that sailed the Great Lakes in the nineteenth century including the *David Dows,* the only five-masted sailing ship to operate on the Great Lakes. There are also photographs of ferries and overnight steamers, such as the *Tashmoo* and the *City of Detroit III,* that took people on weekend cruises in the early twentieth century. The many freighters that sail the Great Lakes today and those that are now gone are well represented. Included are the 1,000 foot *Roger Blough* and the ill-fated *Edmund Fitzgerald* that sank in a storm on 10 November 1975, with all hands lost.

The Michigan section of the picture catalog is larger than the Great Lakes section. Its greatest asset lies in pictures of Michigan localities with diverse subjects ranging from airviews to weather.

The Detroit section of the picture catalog is the strongest, containing approximately 35,000 pictures. There are artists' renderings of Detroit from as early as 1701, the year the city was founded by Antoine de la Mothe Cadillac; an original watercolor of the city in 1794, as well as hundreds of photographs and drawings of Detroit's churches from the earliest wooden buildings (St. Anne's, 1701) to the sturdy marble, granite, and stone churches of the twentieth century. There are hundreds of photographs of businesses in the city. Also depicted are newsworthy events such as the departure of the First Michigan Regiment that left to fight in the Civil War on 11 May 1861. In addition to the

5 DETROIT–STREETS–WOODWARD: Woodward Avenue, Detroit, looking north, *ca.,* 1890. The street was named for Augustus B. Woodward, Judge of Michigan Territory, 1805-24.

6 Woodward Avenue, Detroit, looking north, *ca.* 1920.

7 Original water color painting of Detroit in 1794, called the "Lady Astor Picture" because it was discovered in a small shop in Plymouth, England, in 1923 by Lady Astor and given to the library.

8 *City of Detroit III.* Built in Toledo in 1912, this side-wheel passenger steamer was said to be the largest of its kind in the world when built. It was dismantled in Detroit in 1956.

subjects listed above, the Detroit section includes pictures of monuments, organizations, schools, streets, to name but a few. One of the more interesting collections comes under the subject heading COS- TUME, which directs the researcher to pictures of people in everyday clothes, giving a fascinating view of changing fashions, styles, tastes, and social mores during the late nineteenth and early twentieth century.

### Detroit Chronology (No. 7)

This catalog is a chronological file of events and activities that occurred in Detroit from 1603 to 1950. It is very specific, and an event and its cor- responding date are recorded on each card. It includes such important events as the founding of Detroit by Antoine de la Mothe Cadillac on 23 July 1701, not to mention notable events in a decade, such as the installa- tion of the first bathtub in Detroit in 1848.

### Wayne County Coroners' Files (No. 8)

This is not a roll of death records. It is an alphabetically arranged file of cards listing information on people who died in Wayne County under circumstances that made it necessary for a coroner to be called in to the case. In each file, the name, residency, occupation, death date, age, birthplace, sex, race, and marital status of the deceased is listed. The catalog covers the period of ca. 1870-1888.

### Newspaper Chronology (No. 9)

This file contains references to Detroit and Michigan newspapers held by the Burton Collection. It is divided into two parts. One covers Detroit; the other covers Michigan. Under each section the cards are ar- ranged chronologically and lists newspapers by month and year. The Detroit section includes newspapers published in Detroit from 1809 to 1986. The Michigan section includes newspapers published in other Michigan cities from 1825 to 1973. For example, the Detroit section contains cards for the *Michigan Essay or Impartial Observer,* which published only one issue dated 31 August 1809, and the *Democratic Free Press and Michigan Intelligencer*, which began publication on 5 May 1831, and continues today as the *Detroit Free Press.*

### Genealogical Index (No. 10)

This is an alphabetical catalog of references to articles in magazines and books that deal with specific family names. It contains references to one family in other family histories or in other genealogical sources. All sources referred to in the catalog are in the Burton Collection. For example, it would have references to the Armstrong family that appeared in the Hamlin family history or vice versa. It is important to remember this distinction. One will not find listed here references to a family in its own family history, meaning that, if researchers looked under the Armstrong family, they would not locate books that are completely dedicated to the Armstrong family. They would only find those books listed in the Burton Main Catalog (No.1).

The Genealogical Index is unique. Rarely do librarians have the time to create an index of many of their genealogical sources quite like this one. The author is aware of a similar index at the Newberry Library, but, otherwise, very few of these extensive genealogical indexes of library sources exist.

### Coats of Arms (No. 11)

Here are listed references to pictures and descriptions of coats of arms arranged alphabetically by name. The pictures may be in color or black and white and may be found in books, magazines, and newspapers.

### Vital Records (No. 12)

In this catalog, the researcher will find references to census records, birth, marriage, and death records, cemetery inscriptions, tax lists, wills, probate records, and other registers and lists. The catalog is arranged alphabetically by country, then by the next smallest governmental unit such as state or province. Under the state or province, the arrangement is by city and county and is interfiled alphabetically. Under each foreign country, the references are arranged alphabetically by county, or, in the case of Canada, by province, then by county. England, Ireland, and Scotland have entries, such as Sussex County or Lancaster County, interfiled with cities such as Canterbury or London. References for Canada are listed first under the name of the province, such as Ontario or Quebec; then references to Windsor, Ontario, and Essex County, Ontario, are interfiled alphabetically. The references to the different American states follow the same arrangement as described above. Alabama would be listed first with all references to cities and counties in Alabama interfiled alphabetically together. It would be followed by Arkansas through to the last state, Wyoming.

**Military Service Lists (No. 13)**

Often genealogists want to know whether one of their ancestors served in a particular war. This catalog contains references to lists of people who served in the military during wars fought both in North America and by the United States. The references cover the Colonial Wars from the Pequot War (1636-38) down to the Vietnam War.

It is arranged chronologically by war, then by state, and then by county. For example, a researcher looking to see if an ancestor from Wayne County, Michigan, had served in the Civil War would look under Michigan, and then under Wayne County. There they would find references to lists of men who served in the Civil War from Wayne County, Michigan.

**DSGR Charts (No. 14)**

The Detroit Society for Genealogical Research (DSGR) has met, under the auspices of the Burton Collection, at the Detroit Main Library since its formation over fifty years ago. As its name indicates, it is dedicated to the study of genealogy. It assists persons in doing their own genealogy and encourages genealogical research.

At one time, those who wanted to join the society were required to submit a genealogical chart. This has not been true for several years, but the society still maintains those charts and encourages its members to submit their charts even today.

This catalog is an alphabetically arranged index to the names found in the DSGR charts. The society itself maintains this file and adds to it regularly as they receive new charts. Each chart is given a number, such as "H-13" for the Hamlin chart. All references to names in the Hamlin chart have the H-13 code on the card. For example, a researcher may be looking for the Avery family and while looking under Avery finds a reference to "Hamlin Chart H-13." This would mean the researcher should ask for the Hamlin Chart H-13, and in it they will find references to the Avery family.

This catalog is an excellent source of information on specific families. Someone else has already done the work. As a researcher, take advantage of it.

**Detroit and Michigan Biography Index (No. 15)**

Researchers looking for information on people who lived or died in Detroit or Michigan must use this catalog. It is arranged alphabetically by last name. It includes information on the actual cards or references to information in books, magazines, pamphlets, newspapers, and other printed sources. For example, if a researcher were interested in biographical information on Clarence M. Burton, they would look under his last name. There would be cards giving references to portions of books on Mr. Burton, articles in magazines and newspapers, and a newspaper clipping file on Mr. Burton.

Photographs of individuals are referred to in this catalog. The photographs are not listed separately in the file but are generally found with the newspaper clippings on that individual. For example, researchers looking for photographs of Gerald Ford, former United States President and Michigan congressman, would look under his last name. They would probably find a card bearing the words "See Reading Room File." They would then fill out a slip with those exact words and take it to the desk in the Reading Room. The file would be brought up and would contain all the newspaper clippings and photographs on Gerald Ford.

## Special Designations in the Catalogs and Call Numbers

The researcher must know about certain designations used with the call numbers on the cards in the catalogs previously listed within this chapter. Each designation represents a special category of material in the Burton Collection. All the designations are considered part of the call number for the item. It is very important to write down the designations with the call number on the card, for without them the item number will be incomplete. All the items with these designations, except the "L" items, are found in the closed basement stacks and must be requested at the Reference Desk in the Reading Room. These designations are:

**L:** oversize. Books that are larger than a normal size book. Some of these are shelved in certain areas in the Reading Room which will be discussed later. Some **L** items are also in the basement stacks.

**XL:** extra oversize. Books even larger than those with the **L** designation.

**Excerpts and Miscellania (E & M):** newspaper clippings on subjects and individuals.

**Reserved Section:** books valuable because of their rarity.

**Pamphlet Section:** pamphlets on various subjects.

**Maps:** maps of various geographical areas.

**Prints:** photographs, drawings, lithographs, pictures of various subjects.

**Negatives:** negatives of photographs.

**Glass Negatives:** negatives of photographs printed on glass.

**Lantern Slides:** similar to glass negatives but designed to be used in an earlier machine similar to the slide projector of today.

**Daguerreotypes:** the earliest photographs which were printed on a light-sensitive silver-coated metallic plate.

**Cuts:** wooden blocks with pictures cut into them used in old printing processes.

**Reading Room File:** newspaper clippings and photograph files once kept in the Reading Room but now stored in the closed basement stacks.

**Scrapbooks (SB):** scrapbooks of newspaper clippings.

**Microfilm and Microfiche:** types of microforms in the Burton Collection.

### Call Numbers Used on the Books

The call numbers used on the books in the Burton Collection are based on the Dewey decimal system developed by Melville Dewey. Mr. Dewey created a number system whereby all knowledge would be assigned a three digit number between 001 and 999. For example, American history was assigned the number 973-979.8.

Each call number includes a top line that is the Dewey number and a bottom line that is called a Cutter number. The bottom line is a system developed by Charles A. Cutter. It is a number system based on the last name of the author of the book.

The Burton Collection contains virtually every number in the Dewey decimal system, but the majority of the books fall within the History number 900-999. Mr. Dewey assigned the numbers 974-979.8 to regions of the United States, designating one number for each state. For example, the Dewey number for the history of New England is 974, and the number for Maine is 974.1, New Hampshire 974.2, Vermont 974.3, through the remainder of the New England states. Each region in the United States is treated in the same way.

In the Burton Collection, each state is divided into three basic parts: general history of the state, county histories, and town histories. Several examples using a fictitious book title and author are given below. The general histories have a number such as:

*History of Maine* by John Armstrong
974.1 (Dewey)
A435 (Cutter)

The histories of counties have the number of the state immediately followed by a lower case letter, the first letter of the name of the county. For example:

*History of Green County, Maine* by John Armstrong
974.1g5
A435

The histories of towns will have the number of the state immediately followed by an upper case letter. That letter is the first letter of the name of the town. For example:

*History of Portland, Maine* by John Armstrong
974.1P6
A435

Within the histories of the states, counties, and cities, books may be broken down by subject. Generally speaking, the subjects are related to the field of genealogy. When books are broken down by subject, a third line is used. The top line is the Dewey number, the second line is the subject, and the third line is the Cutter number. In these cases the 97 is dropped from the top line. The early staff of the Burton Collection began this practice, and it has been continued to the present day. Whenever a three line number appears on a catalog card in the Burton Collection, the 97 will be dropped from the number. For example:

*Vital Records of Maine* by John Armstrong
41 (Dewey)
929.3 (subject)
A435 (Cutter)

*Vital Records of Green County, Maine* by John Armstrong
41g5
929.3
A435

*Vital Records of Portland, Maine* by John Armstrong
41P6
929.3
A435.

# The Reading Room

The floor plans of the Reading Room are included (see pages *xiii* and *xiv*) to give the researcher an idea of how the book stacks are set up in the room. There are thirteen tables for researchers on the first floor and fourteen researchers' tables on the balcony. These tables are not shown on the diagrams due to space constraints within the diagrams.

All the stacks in the Reading Room are open. This means that researchers are free to take any of the books from the stacks and use them at tables in the room without first requesting the books from librarians.

All books and magazines on a particular state are shelved together. All books and magazines on counties and towns within a state are shelved together in alphabetical order.

The floor plan of the main floor of the Reading Room depicts the book stacks as they are in this room. The call numbers on the book stacks on the floor plan are the same as they appear on the stacks. As the researcher can see, the books are arranged by Dewey decimal numbers beginning with 974 (New England) and going through 977.4 (Michigan). Most of the individual genealogies (929.2) are shelved alphabetically on the outer walls in the Reading Room, but some are shelved in the closed stacks in the basement. In the same vein, most of the state, county, and town histories are shelved in the Reading Room, but some are shelved in the basement. For both these categories, the best course would be first to check the shelves in the Reading Room, and, if the book cannot be located, the call slip should be taken to the Reference Desk. The librarian will have the book brought up from the basement.

The census indexes are shelved on the south wall of the Reading Room next to the "new books" shelves. Current issues of several genealogical magazines are shelved behind the two Reference Desks.

The balcony above the main floor of the Reading Room contains the remainder of the Dewey decimal numbers for the United States, foreign countries, and a collection of material on Abraham Lincoln designated the Edgar Dewitt Jones Lincoln Collection. The balcony books actually begin on the south side with bibliographies (016). The remainder of the states from 977.5 (Wisconsin) to 979.7 (Washington) are on the balcony. Books on foreign countries are found on the north side of the balcony beginning with Scotland (941), continuing through the British Isles (942), continental Europe (943-49), Canada (971), and the Caribbean (972). These books on the south side of the balcony also use the same break down as the United States: general history of the country, county histories, and city histories. They also use the designations of small letters for counties and capital letters for towns as described under "Call Numbers Used on Books" (see page 17).

# 3
# Special Subjects and Materials

## Indexes

Indexes to large groups of materials of various kinds can be very helpful and timesaving to genealogists. The largest index is the *American Genealogical – Biographical Index* by Fremont Rider. Two series have been published, referred to here as Series One and Two. The first was published between 1942 and 1952. It covers forty-eight volumes and includes some two million entries indexed from over 200 works. The majority of the works indexed were genealogies as well as biographical sources, local history materials, and the 1790 United States Census. The set is arranged alphabetically by surname and includes the first name, approximate birth year, state, source, and page number.

The second series of the *American Genealogical – Biographical Index*, was begun in 1952 and is not yet complete. At present, 147 volumes have been published, the latest entry being that for Shirley Robertson. The second series is projected to include twelve million entries indexed from over 1,100 sources. This series is arranged the same way as the first series, and the same information is given. Series Two includes all entries and sources from Series One, plus added sources such as all the genealogical queries submitted to the *Boston Transcript,* a newspaper published from the late 1890s to the 1930s.

*Index to American Genealogies* published in 1900 by Joel Munsell and Sons is another index genealogists should consult. Though it is out of date, there is much valuable information offered. This work, with its supplement published in 1908, indexes genealogies, town histories, county histories, historical society publications, biographies, and genealogical and historical magazines. Arranged alphabetically by surname, the nearly 50,000 entries list the title of the work and the relevant page numbers. In one book, a genealogist can discover if any of his ancestors are to be found in over 200 other books.

Another general index is the *Index to Genealogical Periodicals* by Donald Lines Jacobus. This work indexes sixty-two periodicals, historical society proceedings, collections, and papers published from the nineteenth century through 1952. It is actually three volumes bound together in a single book, and the Burton Collection's copy is a reprint published in 1978. There are sections on surnames, places, and subjects. Each entry gives the surname, the place of the subject, the source, and page number.

A more recent periodical index is the *Genealogical Periodical Annual Index.* Begun in 1962, this work indexes over 244 genealogical periodicals as they are issued. It is arranged by surname and gives the full name, birthdate, locality or country, and source of information. The Burton Collection holds issues through 1985.

A few large genealogical libraries have published indexes to specific parts of their collections. The largest of these is a *Dictionary Catalog of the Local History and Genealogy Division* published by the Research Libraries of the New York Public Library. This eighteen-volume set published in 1974 includes all of the cards from this division's catalog. Entries are filed alphabetically under family name, subjects, and places. The importance of this catalog to the genealogist is that it allows one to locate information on a particular family in a specific book, then with the title of the book, one can determine whether the Burton Collection owns the same book.

An index dealing with a section of a genealogical library is the *Genealogical Index of the Newberry Library,* 1960. This four-volume work indexes all surnames (principally United States families) that appear in the books and historical and genealogical magazines held by the Newberry Library.

The index covers materials published between 1896-1918. There are over 683,000 entries arranged alphabetically by surname, giving the title of the book or magazine and the pages on which the name is to be found.

Still another suggested index is the *Greenlaw Index of the New England Historic Genealogical Society.* This two-volume work published in 1979 includes over 35,000 entries arranged alphabetically by family name in sources found in the society's collections. All works indexed were printed after 1900. This work originally was a card file done by the society's librarian, William Prescott Greenlaw, up to his retirement in 1929 and continued by others until 1940. This work is based on town and county histories, the *New England Historical and Genealogical Register,* the *New York Genealogical and Biographical Record,* and the *Essex Institute Historical Collections.* All these items are in the society's library. There is an entry for any family carried through three generations in a particular work. Each entry lists the surname and first name of a principal ancestor, main towns in which the family resided, the time period involved, source, and date of publication.

Perhaps the most comprehensive index of genealogical information in existence is the *International Genealogical Index (IGI)*. This is a microfiche index of the names found in the computerized files of the Church of Jesus Christ of Latter-day Saints (LDS). Formerly called the *Computer File Index,* the 1984 edition of the *IGI* contains over 88 million names from records of over ninety countries. It includes only persons who are deceased and covers the 1500s to about 1875 with some more recent records. The sources for the records indexed in the *IGI* come from three different areas: first, original or compiled records of births, christenings, and marriages extracted and indexed in the LDS Church extraction program; second, forms submitted by LDS Church members with information on their ancestors; third, LDS temple records.

The *IGI* is arranged by country, then alphabetically by the name of the individual. For each name, the spouse's name is given if the event bears marital connotation (birth, marriage, death, census, will, or probate), date of event, place of event, county, town, or parish, and source in the LDS records. Records in the data base are listed in the *Parish and Vital Records Listing* which is on another microfiche. The *IGI* should be checked by each genealogist in order to ascertain whether work has already been done on their family line. A work of this magnitude is an excellent source that richly rewards the genealogist's time.

## Bibliographies

The Burton Collection holds many bibliographies on various subjects relating to genealogy. Some list books on particular states or specific subjects. It is recommended that the researcher check the Burton Main Catalog (No. 1) to see whether there is a bibliography relevant to their state or subject.

There are a few basic bibliographies that of which researchers should be aware. *Genealogies in the Library of Congress* is a two-volume work arranged alphabetically by family name, giving all the basic information on each genealogy and the Library of Congress call number. Two supplements were published that cover the years 1972-86.

In addition to the supplements, a *Complement to the Genealogies in the Library of Congress (1981)* includes 20,000 entries covering genealogies held by forty-five libraries other than the Library of Congress.

*United States Local Histories in the Library of Congress* is a five-volume work that is a detailed list of books covering local history, state history, town and county history, gazetteers, and collected genealogies. These are only a few of the types of books found in the bibliography. The work is arranged by regions of the country and is an excellent source through which to determine whether a history exists for a particular locality in the United States.

The National Society of the Daughters of the American Revolution (DAR) has published a work similar to those published by the Library of Congress. The *DAR Library Catalog* is actually a two-volume set. The first volume, entitled *Family Histories and Genealogies,* is arranged alphabetically by family name and includes both author and surname indexes. The second volume, *State and Local Histories and Records,* is arranged by state and has author and surname indexes. Aside from local histories, it includes biographies, land records, military records, vital records, and wills.

# Periodicals

The Burton Collection subscribes to approximately 550 magazines or periodicals. The magazines included in this number are current issues. In addition, there are several hundred other magazines held by the collection that are no longer published.

The magazines concentrate on the topics of history and genealogy. The coverage of history may be general in nature, such as *American Heritage,* or specific, such as the *Detroit Historical Society Bulletin.* The genealogical magazines, however, are not limited to a particular area when it comes to articles, as are many of the historical magazines. For example, the *Detroit Historical Society Bulletin* includes only articles on or related to Detroit history, whereas the *Detroit Society for Genealogical Research Magazine* includes family histories from all over the United States, church records from churches other than those in Detroit, and birth, marriage, and death records from places other than Detroit.

The magazines are listed alphabetically under their names in the Burton Main Catalog (No. 1). The genealogy magazines are also listed in the same catalog under the heading GENEALOGY – PERIODICALS.

Once a researcher locates a card bearing the name of the magazine in the Burton Main Catalog, he is likely to see printed at the center of the card the words "For Number of Volumes in Library See Check List." This directs one to look in the Check List (No. 2) that lists all the volumes and years which the Burton Collection holds of a particular magazine. From the Check List card, the researcher would write down the call number, located in the top left-hand corner, along with the volume and years required. Many of the state genealogical magazines are shelved with books for the relevant state in the Reading Room. The librarian will either direct the researcher to the material in the Reading Room or have it brought up from the basement stacks. Current issues of several genealogical and historical magazines are kept in the Reading Room for browsing by researchers.

The majority of the magazines that the Burton Collection receives are indexed by the staff. This means that when an issue arrives, a staff member makes a card for each historical or genealogical article, and the cards are filed in the catalogs. For example, in the March 1987 issue of *The American Genealogist,* there may be an article on the Whitney Family. The staff member would type a card giving the call number and name of the magazine, the title of the article, the issue of the magazine, and the pages on which the article is to be found. The card would then be filed in the Genealogical Index (No. 10) under the Whitney Family.

Most of the indexing done in the current genealogy magazines concerns family histories, coats of arms, vital records, and military records. Generally, the cards are filed in catalogs 10 through 13.

If a person is researching a particular state or area, it is a good idea to determine which current and out of print historical and genealogical magazines have published articles on the state or area of interest. Many researchers have found articles on their families published in state historical or local genealogical magazines. One can never be certain that articles on one's family do not exist unless the various, relevant magazines have been consulted.

Nationally, there are several ongoing genealogical magazines. *The American Genealogist* and the *National Genealogical Society Quarterly* along with *The Genealogical Helper* are three of the most popular. The Burton Collection holds all the issues of these magazines. The oldest genealogical magazine in the United States is the *New England Historical and Genealogical Register* which was first published in 1847. The Burton Collection also holds all the issues of this magazine. An excellent source of pictures of coats of arms is *Americana,* a magazine published during the years 1906-43. The DAR has published a magazine called the *DAR Magazine* since 1892, and it is an excellent source of genealogical information, especially on burial places of Revolutionary War soldiers.

Many of the regions of the United States are covered in genealogical magazines, and each state and many towns and counties also publish genealogical magazines. The Burton Collection has a large collection of these magazines. Magazines covering particular regions and states will be discussed further under those regions and states.

# Genealogies

There are approximately 13,500 separate genealogies in the Burton Collection. They include single and multivolume works. Most of these genealogies are shelved on the walls of the main floor of the Reading Room. The researcher can locate the genealogies in the Burton Main Catalog (No. 1) under the family name, such as "Armstrong Family." Cards with this heading represent books about the Armstrong family.

These genealogies often begin with the earliest ancestor the author could locate and move forward to the author, then children, or grandchildren.

Many of the genealogies have been indexed in the Genealogical Index (No. 10). Years ago when the Burton Collection had more staff, any genealogy with ten entries in its index under another name than the basic name of the genealogy would have a card made for the Genealogical Index. The card would be filed under the name of the other family with the call number of the book and the pages of the entries on the card. A fictitious example will illustrate this:

929.2  Hamilton Family
A435  Armstrong, John
*The Armstrong Family in America*
1702-1920 p. 102-12

This indicates that on pages 102-12 in *The Armstrong Family in America* there are listings for the Hamilton family. A researcher should write down the call number (929.2 A435) and look for the book on the walls of the main floor Reading Room. If it was not possible to locate the book, the call number should be taken to the Reference Desk where the book would be brought up from the basement stacks.

The staff of the Burton Collection is now too small and the work load too great to index genealogies any longer. However, genealogical articles in magazines are indexed by the Burton staff (see Periodicals) and entries are put into the Genealogical Index (No. 10).

# Censuses

The United States census has been taken every ten years since 1790. It was done geographically by counties within states and then by townships within counties. From 1790-1840 the census takers were instructed to write down  only the name of the head of the family. The remaining people in the house were recorded as numbers in columns under male, female, and slaves. An example would be:

| | Males | | Females | |
|---|---|---|---|---|
| | Under 5/5 – 10/10 – 15/15 – 20/ | | /Under 5/5 – 10/10 – 15/15 – 20 | |
| **John Lee** | 1 | 1 | 1 | 1 |

This table shows that in 1840 in the house of John Lee there was one son under 5, one daughter under 5, John Lee (males 15 – 20), and his wife (female 15 – 20).

In 1790 there were only four columns: the males under 16, males 16 and up, females, and slaves, but by 1840 the columns were broken down by every five years.

In 1850 the census began to record everyone in the household by name, including their age, sex, color, occupation, and value of real estate. The place of birth was recorded by state, if in the United States, or by foreign country. In each census year certain other information was included. By 1880 the relationship to the head of the family and the place of birth of the parents were included. In 1900 people born outside the United States were being asked the year they had come to this country and whether they were citizens; also, how long they had been married, their month and year of birth, how many children the woman had borne, and how many were living. A good discussion of the United States Census with illustrations of the schedules can be found in *The Researchers Guide to American Genealogy* by Val Greenwood and *The Source* by Arlene Eakle and Johni Cerny.

The Burton Collection holds the United States Census for each state in America from 1790 to 1900 and is presently buying the 1910 census for each state. The 1890 census was destroyed by a fire in 1921.

As was mentioned earlier, the United States Census was done geographically. This means that the census taker went from house to house. He would travel down a street and record the names of everyone who lived there. The problem here is that there is no way to find an individual without searching name by name through a specific geographical area. The genealogist has been saved this extensive searching thanks to the existence of indexes – at least, for the earlier census years. The 1790 census has been printed and indexed completely. Also, there are printed editions of censuses for various states for various years. Many state or local genealogical societies have published indexes of their early censuses after 1790. For example, Michigan has indexes for 1820, 1830, 1840, and 1850. Thanks to Accelerated Indexing Systems, all the states for 1850 have been indexed, and they are working on 1860 and 1870.

These indexes include only the name of the head of the family, the county and township, and the page number in the census. The indexes that the Burton Collection holds are found in the Vital Records Catalog (No. 12) under STATE-CENSUS (YEAR)-INDEXES, i.e., MICHIGAN-CENSUS-1840-INDEXES. These are shelved on the south wall of the Reading Room.

The following lists printed indexes to censuses available in the Burton Collection:

ALABAMA 1850, 1860
ARIZONA 1860, 1864, 1870
ARKANSAS 1860
CALIFORNIA 1850, 1860
CONNECTICUT 1800, 1850
DELAWARE 1850, 1860
DISTRICT OF COLUMBIA 1820, 1850, 1860
FLORIDA 1840, 1850, 1860
GEORGIA 1820, 1830 1850, 1860
ILLINOIS 1830, 1840, 1850, 1860
INDIANA 1840, 1850, 1860
IOWA 1850
KENTUCKY 1810, 1820, 1830, 1840, 1850
LOUISIANA 1850, 1860
MAINE 1850
MARYLAND 1800, 1820, 1840, 1850
MASSACHUSETTS 1800, 1850
MICHIGAN 1710 – 1830, 1840, 1850, 1860 (WAYNE COUNTY)
MINNESOTA 1850
MISSISSIPPI 1850, 1860
MISSOURI 1830, 1840, 1850, 1860
NEBRASKA 1860
NEVADA 1910
NEW HAMPSHIRE 1800, 1850, 1860
NEW JERSEY 1850, 1860
NEW YORK 1800, 1810, 1820, 1830, 1840, 1850, 1860
NORTH CAROLINA 1800, 1810, 1850
OHIO 1820, 1830, 1840, 1850, 1860
OREGON 1880
PENNSYLVANIA 1800, 1810, 1850, 1860
RHODE ISLAND 1850, 1860, 1870
SOUTH CAROLINA 1850, 1860
TENNESSEE 1850, 1860, 1870

TEXAS 1850, 1860
UTAH 1850, 1860, 1870
VERMONT 1800, 1850, 1860
VIRGINIA 1810, 1820, 1830, 1850
WEST VIRGINIA 1880
WISCONSIN 1850

The United States Census Bureau has done indexes for the 1880, 1900, and 1910 censuses. They are structured on a coding of the last name of the head of the family in the census. The coding is based on the sound of the last name, and the index is called the Soundex. Consonants are coded with a number from 1 to 6. Vowels are dropped. The Soundex number begins with the first letter of the last name and is only three digits long, no matter how long the name is. An example of the author's last name will suffice:

OLDENBURG
4 3  5
*Soundex for Oldenburg O – 435*

The Burton Collection holds only the Soundex index for the United States. censuses for Michigan for 1880, 1900, and 1910.

## Michigan Census

In addition to the United States censuses for Michigan for 1820 to 1910 on microfilm, the Burton Collection also holds part of the 1810 Michigan federal census, the 1827 Michigan territorial census in printed form, and a state census for Wayne County, Michigan, done in 1884. The 1810 census is the original handwritten census and is found in the Benjamin F. H. Witherell Papers. It includes only the District of Detroit which included the city and ten miles of the Detroit river front north and south of the city. It lists the name of the head of the family only. The other people in the household were listed under sex and in categories or age groups such as males under 10, 10-16, 16-26, 26-45, over 45. Females, free colored persons, and slaves were listed in the same categories as the males. This census appears to be all that has survived of the 1810 federal census of Michigan. It is also published in the *Detroit Society for Genealogical Research Magazine* [12 (Fall 1968): 17-23], and again in *Michigan Censuses 1710-1830* by Donna Valley Russell (pages 87-91, 100).

The 1827 territorial census of Michigan is published in the *Michigan Pioneer and Historical Collection,* Vol. 12 (1887). The categories are basically the same as those of the 1810 census listed above.

The remainder of the 1827 territorial census was published in the *Detroit Society for Genealogical Research Magazine* [19 (Winter 1955): 51-57]. The complete 1827 census is published in *Michigan Censuses 1710-1830* (pages 149-60).

Beginning in 1854, the state of Michigan took a census every ten years. This ceased in 1904. Very few of the state schedules have survived. One that did was the 1884 census of Wayne County, Michigan. It is to be found in the Wayne County Archives in the Burton Collection. The census includes all the townships of the county but not the city of Detroit. It listed the name of every person in the household, place of birth, relationship to the head of the family, age, sex, occupation, and years of residence in the United States.

# Canadian Censuses

The Burton Collection holds several Canadian censuses. Of the Ontario censuses, it holds those for 1842, 1848, 1850, 1851, 1861, 1871, 1881, and 1891. The Quebec census is held for 1851, 1861, and 1881. In addition, the Burton Collection has New Brunswick (1881) and Nova Scotia (1881). The Canadian census was done geographically and is similar to the United States census. The Provinces are divided into counties and the counties into townships.

The Ontario censuses before 1851 list only the name of the head of the household, and the other persons in the house are listed in columns similar to the United States census of the same period. Beginning in 1851 everyone in the household was listed by name, age, sex, birthplace (province or country), religion, marital status, education, and origin, meaning English, French, and so on.

There are very few indexes available for the Canadian censuses. Some individual county censuses, such as Essex County, Ontario (1851), have been indexed, but generally neither counties nor provinces have been indexed. The indexes that the Burton Collection holds can be found listed in the Vital Records Catalog (No. 12) under the province name and county, i.e., ONTARIO – ESSEX CO. – CENSUS – 1851 – INDEXES.

# Ship Passenger Lists

The United States National Archives holds unpublished ship passenger arrival lists kept by United States Customs for arrivals at various ports, including New York, 1820-97. The Burton Collection holds microfilm copies of the New York lists for the period of 1820-February 1873. The lists are arranged by date of arrival and name of the ship. The information given also includes the names of passengers, age, sex, occupation, destination by country, former residence (occasionally including state or province) and those who died on the voyage.

There are alphabetical indexes for the New York lists for the period 1820-46 only. This is an excellent means for determining the date upon which an ancestor arrived in the United States. It gives the last name, first name, those who accompanied the person (other family members), age, occupation, nationality, last permanent residence (country), destination (sometimes a specific state), port of entry, name of vessel, and date of arrival in New York. Since there is no index for the years 1847-97, the researcher must look through list after list for ancestors. The only practical way to use the New York lists from 1847 onward is to know at least the year of immigration of an ancestor. If an ancestor was in the United States in 1900 or 1910, the researcher should look for them in the United States census where everyone was asked the year of their immigration to the United States.

There are many published ship passenger lists in books and magazines. The most comprehensive index to these ship passenger lists is *Passenger and Immigration Lists Index* edited by P. William Filby. It is an alphabetical index of published ship passenger lists that covers the period 1600-1900. Under each name, the date of the list is given along with the source, the page in the source, the place of arrival, and age of each passenger. All sources are listed at the front of the book. William Filby's book was published in 1982, and annual supplements have been issued through 1987. With its supplements, the book claims to have indexed 1,250,000 people.

The researcher should be aware that *Passenger and Immigration Lists Index* does not index any of the lists held by the National Archives. Generally, if an ancestor came from Eastern or Western Europe during the period 1820-97 they will only be found on the lists kept by United States Customs. If an ancestor came in an earlier period, the Filby book is the best source.

Another published ship passenger list is the *Famine Immigrants* published by Genealogical Publishing Co. It is a seven-volume work covering the period 1846-51. The seventh volume of this work, covering

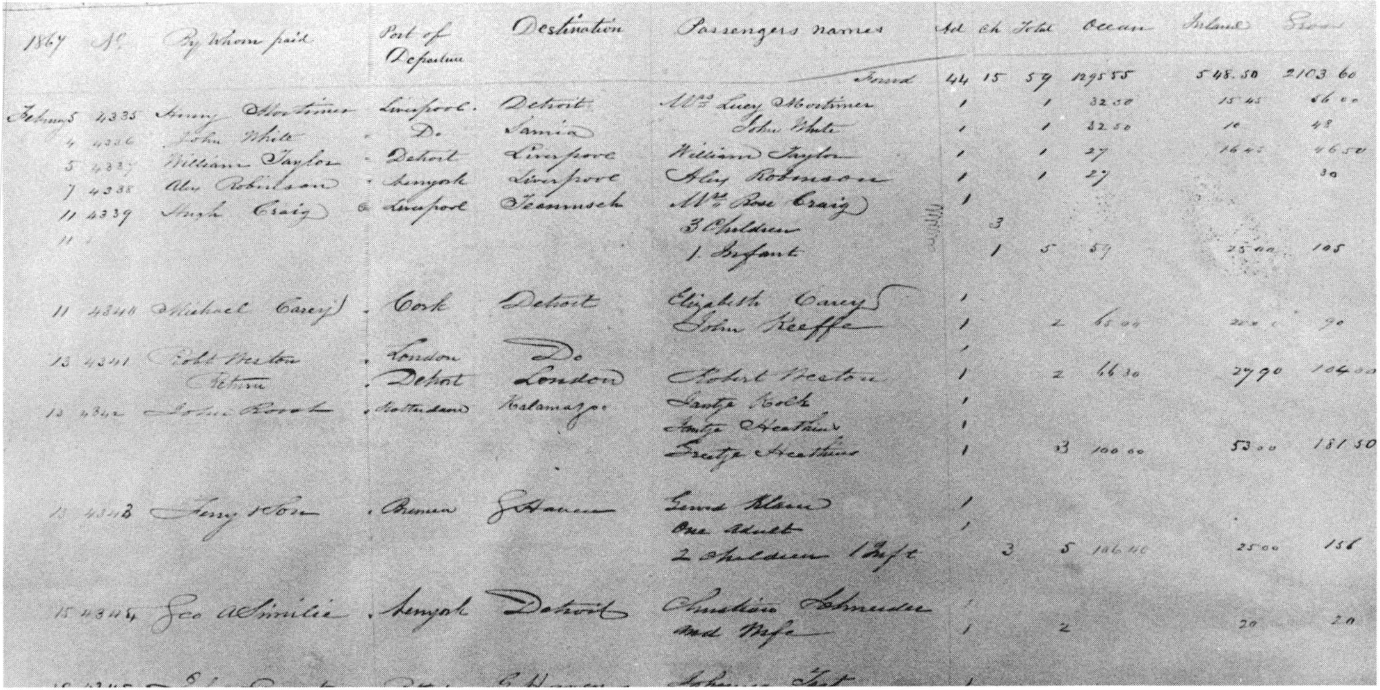

| 1867 | No. | By whom paid | Port of Departure | Destination | Passengers names | Ad | Ch | Total | Ocean | Inland | Gross |
|---|---|---|---|---|---|---|---|---|---|---|---|
| | | | | | Forward | 44 | 15 | 59 | 1295 55 | 548.50 | 2103 60 |
| Feby 5 | 4335 | Henry Mortimer | Liverpool | Detroit | Mrs Lucy Mortimer | 1 | | 1 | 32 50 | 15 45 | 56 00 |
| 4 | 4336 | John White | Do | Sarnia | John White | 1 | | 1 | 32 50 | 10 | 48 |
| 5 | 4337 | William Taylor | Detroit | Liverpool | William Taylor | 1 | | 1 | 27 | 16 45 | 46 50 |
| 7 | 4338 | Alex Robinson | Newyork | Liverpool | Alex Robinson | 1 | | 1 | 27 | | 30 |
| 11 | 4339 | Hugh Craig | Liverpool | Tecumseh | Mrs Rose Craig | 1 | | | | | |
| | | | | | 3 Children | | 3 | | | | |
| 11 | | | | | 1 Infant | | 1 | 5 | 57 | 25 00 | 105 |
| 11 | 4340 | Michael Carey | Cork | Detroit | Elizabeth Carey | 1 | | | | | |
| | | | | | John Keeffe | 1 | | 2 | 65 00 | 20 00 | 90 |
| 13 | 4341 | Robt Weston | London | Do | | 1 | | | | | |
| | | Return | Detroit | London | Robert Weston | 1 | | 2 | 66 30 | 27 90 | 104 00 |
| 13 | 4342 | John Root | Rotterdam | Kalamazoo | Jantje Kolk | 1 | | | | | |
| | | | | | Antje Heathien | 1 | | | | | |
| | | | | | Grietje Heathien | 1 | | 3 | 100 00 | 53 00 | 181 50 |
| 13 | 4343 | Ferry & Son | Bremen | G Haven | [illegible] | 1 | | | | | |
| | | | | | One Adult | 1 | | | | | |
| | | | | | 2 Children 1 Inft | | 3 | 5 | 186 40 | 25 00 | 156 |
| 15 | 4344 | Geo A Smilie | Newyork | Detroit | Christian Schneider | 1 | | | | | |
| | | | | | and Wife | 1 | | 2 | | 20 | 20 |

9 Passage Register found in the Richard R. Elliott Papers.

March 1851-December 1851, has not yet appeared. The publishers took the list of passenger arrivals at New York for the period listed above and abstracted the names that werc Irish or those passengers who embarked from an Irish port. The ship lists are arranged by date, and there is an alphabetical index in each volume. The lists give the name of the ship, the names of passengers, age, sex, port and date of embarkation, and date of arrival.

The *Hamburg Lists* are another sort of ship's passenger list. They were kept by officials at the German port to record passengers from Hamburg to the United States. There are the direct lists, which include those who sailed directly from Hamburg to their destination (generally New York), and the indirect lists, which include those who sailed from Hamburg but stopped at one port before they reached the United States.

The Burton Collection holds the direct lists for 1850-72 and the indirect lists 1855-73. There are indexes for both lists. The lists themselves generally give the name of each passenger, age, sex, former country of residence, former occupation, and destination (country or state in the United States). Many times the *Hamburg Lists* will give the province or town of origin; therefore, they are a very good source for researchers who are trying to find information on the town of origin of European immigrants.

## Immigration and Naturalization Records

The Burton Collection does not hold any true immigration records as kept by the United States Customs Service to record the entrance of immigrants into the United States. Although Detroit · is across the Detroit River from Windsor, Ontario, Canada, no immigration records were kept before the creation of the United States Immigration and Naturalization Service in 1906. Records since 1906 are kept at the United States Immigration and Naturalization Service in Washington, D.C.

The Burton Collection does hold the naturalization, or citizenship, papers of individuals who applied for and were granted citizenship at Detroit Recorders Court for the period 1852-1906. The papers include the Declaration of Intent, or First Papers, that were filed by persons requesting to become citizens. After a period of time (generally three years) the Second Papers, or Oath of Allegiance, were filed and the individuals were then declared United States citizens.

The papers gave the name of the individual and the date on which the papers were filed. Generally speaking, the papers did not include

The Detroit Courier Print, 44 West Larned Street.

# DECLARATION OF INTENTION.

[ COPY. ]

STATE OF MICHIGAN } ss.
COUNTY OF WAYNE.

*The Circuit Court for said County, to wit:*

I, *Frederick Rapp* do

solemnly swear that it is bona fide my intention to become a CITIZEN OF THE UNITED

STATES, and to RENOUNCE FOREVER, all allegiance and fidelity to each and

every Foreign Prince, Potentate, State or Sovereignty whatsoever, and particularly

WILLIAM II, EMPEROR OF GERMANY, of whom I have been a subject.

Sworn to and Subscribed before me at

Detroit, this

day of *April* A. D., 189 *4*

*C. N. Austin Deputy* Clerk.

(Signed.) *Frederick Rapp*

STATE OF MICHIGAN, } ss.
COUNTY OF WAYNE.

I, HENRY M. REYNOLDS, Clerk of the Circuit

Court of said County, do certify that the above is a true copy of the original Declara-

tion of Intention of *Frederick Rapp*

to become a CITIZEN OF THE UNITED STATES, remaining of record in my office.

IN TESTIMONY WHEREOF, I have hereunto sub-

scribed my name, and affixed the seal of the said

Court, the *Thirtieth* day of

*April* one thousand eight hundred and

ninety *four*

*Henry M. Reynolds* Clerk.

By *C. N. Austin* Deputy Clerk.

10  Declaration of Intention of Frederick Rapp.
From the Recorders Court Naturalization Papers.

birthplace but required the individual to disavow allegiance to the ruler of the country of origin. Also, the records did not include information as to when the person immigrated to the United States.

A researcher requesting access to the Recorders Court Naturalization Papers should ask at the Reference Desk in the Reading Room. There is an alphabetical index that can be checked, and the papers for any name on the list will be brought upstairs.

There is one manuscript collection that has some records which are not immigration records per se but which could help researchers tracing Irish immigrants to Michigan. The papers of Richard R. Elliott cover the period 1848-80. Elliott was an immigration agent of sorts who handled correspondence and monetary transactions between Irish immigrants in Michigan and their families or friends in Ireland. His letterbooks of this period have many, many names of Irish immigrants to Michigan. This collection is an excellent source of information for Irish genealogy, but it is not indexed and would have to be searched item by item.

Elliott kept a passage register that covers the years 1851-69. It appears that people in the United States would pay Elliott a fee to arrange passage for their own family or friends. The register lists the date of the transaction, who paid for the passage, the port of departure, port of destination, and the passengers' names. There are many entries for departures from Cork and Liverpool to Detroit and back. The arrangement is by date so the researcher must search the register name by name. Still it is one of the best sources for Irish immigration to Michigan and especially Detroit.

## Military Records

The Burton Collection holds records of those who fought in wars for the United States as far back as 1636 and as recent as the Vietnam War. The best source for finding these records is the Military Records Catalog (No. 13). It is arranged chronologically by war, then by state under each war. The states are then divided by county. Each card represents an article or book with a list of those who served in a particular war from the state or county, i.e., CIVIL WAR–MICHIGAN–WAYNE, COUNTY.

A list of the wars and time periods covered in the Military Records Catalog is given below:

| | |
|---|---|
| PEQUOT WAR | 1636-38 |
| KING PHILIP'S WAR | 1675-76 |
| KING WILLIAM'S WAR | 1689-97 |
| QUEEN ANNE'S WAR | 1702-13 |

| | |
|---|---|
| KING GEORGE'S WAR | 1744-48 |
| FRENCH AND INDIAN WAR | 1755-63 |
| REVOLUTIONARY WAR | 1775-83 |
| 1783-1811 | |
| WAR WITH FRANCE | 1798-1800 |
| WAR OF 1812 | |
| 1815-44 | |
| BLACK HAWK WAR | 1832 |
| WAR WITH MEXICO | 1845-48 |
| CIVIL WAR | 1861-65 |
| WAR OF 1898 | |
| EUROPEAN WAR | 1914-18 |
| WORLD WAR II | 1939-45 |
| VIETNAM WAR | |

The military records are the most complete for the American Revolution, the War of 1812, and the Civil War. Genealogical societies, historical societies, or states themselves have published lists of the individuals who served from their states in the American Revolution. These lists will generally include the person's name and the unit in which he served. Some of the state lists include additional information such as enlistment and discharge dates and whether wounded or killed in battle. Many of the state lists are not indexed so the researcher may have to search through them page by page.

The National Society of the Daughters of the American Revolution has published a work entitled *DAR Patriot Index*. This alphabetical list includes everyone who served in the American Revolution and was used by a members of the DAR to gain entrance into the society. Though it includes both men and women who served in the Revolution, it is not a complete list of veterans. Listed are birth, marriage, death, and dates along with spouses' names. Another aid for finding Revolutionary War soldiers is the National Genealogical Society publication, *Index of Revolutionary War Pension Applications* which gives more information including the pension number.

In addition to the many published books of lists of persons who served in the Revolution, the Burton Collection holds the Revolutionary War Pension and Bounty Land Warrant Applications. These are microfilm copies of original documents at the National Archives. They include all the documents submitted by men, women, and widows of veterans applying for pensions or bounty land based on their service in the Revolutionary War. These records are arranged alphabetically by the name of the veteran and include the application, correspondence, family histories, and often complete war records. If a researcher is searching for any kind of information on a Revolutionary War veteran, a search of the pension applications and bounty land warrants is essential.

The records of those who served in the War of 1812 are very complete. They are found on microfilm in an alphabetical arrangement. The microfilm includes only the record jacket with the veteran's name and the unit in which he served. Although no other information is given, the researcher can send the name and unit to the National Archives, and copies of the complete records of all documents will be sent, for a fee, to the researcher.

The Burton Collection's holdings for Civil War records are very good for the northern states but sparse for the southern states. Virtually all the states that fought on the northern side have published lists of men who fought in the volunteer regiments from their state. These lists are generally arranged by regiment number under either infantry or artillery. Under each regiment, the men are listed by companies, then alphabetically by name. Generally, these lists will include the person's name, dates of enlistment and discharge, and the rank held. Occasionally, the service record may be included stating whether the man was wounded or died in service. Unfortunately, most of these state lists have no indexes so researchers have to look for their ancestors name by name. This can be very tedious since most of the lists are multivolume such as the six-volume Pennsylvania list or the eight-volume Ohio list. The forty-six volume Michigan list is one of the few that has been indexed.

The reason the Burton Collection has very few of the lists of men who served in the Confederate Army is that very few have been published. North Carolina is publishing a list of its men who fought for the Confederacy, but it is one of the few southern states to do that. The best place to find listings of Confederate soldiers is the Burton Collection's Military Service Lists Catalog (No. 13). This file includes reference to any lists that the Burton Collection holds – no matter how incomplete. An excellent source for this type of list is the county history. Whenever possible the Burton staff has indexed county histories and has included their Civil War lists in the Military Service Lists (No. 13).

## Vital Records

In genealogy, vital records are generally defined as birth, marriage, and death records. The Burton Collection has one catalog that contains references to vital records, the Vital Records Catalog (No. 12). This catalog refers to vital records in published sources such as books, magazines, and newspapers. Many state and local genealogical societies have published vital records for particular cities or counties. Generally speaking, these publications are very specific and very early, i.e., *Birth Records from the Archives of Wayne County, Michigan,* by the National Society of the Daughters of the American Revolution. The vital records for each state held by the Burton Collection will be discussed under the particular state later.

It is important for the researcher to bear in mind that each state has passed a law which requires that the vital records of each county be recorded and kept by the county clerk as of a specific date. The effective date for each state varies. Massachusetts required that vital records be kept from 1841. Delaware began in 1847, Michigan in 1867, New York in 1880, Alabama in 1908, North Carolina in 1913, and Georgia in 1919. As one can see, the New England states began to require that vital records be kept about the middle of the nineteenth century. They were followed closely by the Midwest, middle Atlantic states, the West, and the South in the twentieth century.

Before these laws were passed, many cities and counties kept records on their own. This is especially reflected in the good collection of published vital records for Massachusetts cities going as far back as the seventeenth century. Generally, vital records of states, counties, or cities rarely appear in printed form after the effective date of the state law requiring them to be recorded and kept by the county clerk. They are only available from the state, or possibly the city or county, where the birth, marriage, or death occurred. For example, if a researcher were looking for a birth record of an ancestor born in Oakland County, Michigan, in 1880, it would not be in published form in the Burton Collection. It would be available only from the Michigan Department of Health at the state capital in Lansing, Michigan.

# City Directories

The Burton Collection holds extensive files of United States city directories. These directories included everyone who had a residence in a particular city. Generally, only the father was listed as representative of a family as well as those who worked outside the home. Burton has a microfiche collection of all the city directories published in the United States prior to 1860. This collection is described in *Bibliography of American Directories through 1860* by Dorothea N. Spear. The Burton Collection also holds city directories for many cities for the 1861-1901 period. The lists below show which directories are available in the Burton Collection.

*1861-1881*

| | |
|---|---|
| Burlington, Vermont | Norfolk, Virginia |
| Chattanooga, Tennessee | Oakland, California |
| Columbus, Ohio | Omaha, Nebraska |
| Davenport, Iowa | Peoria, Illinois |
| Des Moines, Iowa | Portland, Maine |
| Evansville, Indiana | Portland, Oregon |
| Fall River, Massachusetts | Reading, Pennsylvania |
| Fort Wayne, Indiana | Richmond, Virginia |
| Fort Worth, Texas | Sacramento, California |
| Galveston, Texas | St. Paul, Minnesota |
| Grand Rapids, Michigan | Salt Lake City, Utah |
| Joliet, Illinois | San Antonio, Texas |
| Lexington, Kentucky | Seattle, Washington |
| Lowell, Massachusetts | Topeka, Kansas |
| Manchester, New Hampshire | Troy, New York |
| Minneapolis, Minnesota | Utica, New York |
| Mobile, Alabama | Washington, D.C. |
| Montana | Wilmington, Delaware |
| Nevada Territory | Worcester, Massachusetts |

*1861-1901*

| | |
|---|---|
| Albany, New York | Los Angeles, California |
| Atlanta, Georgia | Louisville, Kentucky |
| Baltimore, Maryland | Memphis, Tennessee |
| Boston, Massachusetts | Milwaukee, Wisconsin |
| Brooklyn, New York | Nashville, Tennessee |
| Buffalo, New York | New Haven, Connecticut |
| Charleston, South Carolina | New York, New York |
| Chicago, Illinois | New Orleans, Louisiana |
| Cincinnati, Ohio | Newark, New Jersey |
| Cleveland, Ohio | Paterson, New Jersey |
| Dallas, Texas | Philadelphia, Pennsylvania |
| Dayton, Ohio | Pittsburgh, Pennsylvania |
| Denver, Colorado | Providence, Rhode Island |
| Detroit, Michigan | Rochester, New York |
| Erie, Pennsylvania | St. Louis, Missouri |
| Harrisburg, Pennsylvania | San Francisco, California |

| | |
|---|---|
| Hartford, Connecticut | Savannah, Georgia |
| Indianapolis, Indiana | Scranton, Pennsylvania |
| Jersey City, New Jersey | Syracuse, New York |
| Kansas City, Missouri | Toledo, Ohio |
| Little Rock, Arkansas | |

## Patriotic and Hereditary Societies

These societies require that their members establish their lineage from someone who lived during a particular period in American history, immigrated to the United States during a particular period, or served in a specific war. The Burton Collection has attempted to collect as many of the published records of these societies as possible. Some examples of the records are proceedings of annual conventions, annual reports, yearbooks, registers of members, and lineage books.

The lineage books provide the best information for genealogists. Generally, these books list an ancestor and their lineage down to the member of the society. For example, the *DAR Lineage Books* include the woman's name, the ancestor's name along with their birth, marriage, and death dates, their spouse, and a brief description of their military service. The lineage from the DAR member back to their Revolutionary War ancestor is also recorded.

The *DAR Lineage Books* were published from 1895-1939 and include the complete lineage of each member who joined from 1890 through to 1939. The set comprises 166 volumes. There is an index for all of the Revolutionary War ancestors mentioned in the *DAR Lineage Books* that provides an excellent means through which to ascertain whether one's Revolutionary War ancestor was used to enter the DAR; also, it may be useful in filling in one's genealogy. The *DAR Patriot Index,* with supplements, includes those who served in the American Revolution and were used by members to qualify for membership in the DAR. This source does not include lineages, but it does give the birth and death date of each Revolutionary War ancestor, the name of their spouse, and the marriage date.

In addition to the *DAR Lineage Books,* the Burton Collection has a thirty-four volume set of lineage books for the National Society of Daughters of Founders and Patriots of America. This organization requires that a woman be able to trace her ancestry to someone who came to the United States between 13 May 1607 and 13 May 1687 (founder) and that they also have an ancestor who gave military, civil service, or some other form of aid during the years of the American Revolution, 1775-83 (patriot). The lineage books for this organization have been indexed, and the index includes name, birth, and death dates for each founder and patriot, also the marriage date and the wife's name.

A companion organization to the Daughters of Founders and Patriots of America is the Order of Founders and Patriots. This organization is restricted to men at least eighteen years old who can trace their lineage back through the male line, from either parent, to an ancestor who settled in the colonies prior to 13 May 1657. There must also be an ancestor in that line who served in a military or civil position during the American Revolution. The Registers of this organization were published in 1902, 1911, 1926, 1940, 1960, and 1980. They include the lineage of members, giving the name of the male ancestor, the birth, marriage, and death dates, with the same information listed for the wife in each generation. The Registers are arranged alphabetically with a separate index of founders and patriots contained in each volume.

Meredith B. Colket's *Founders of Early American Families, Emigrants from Europe 1607-57* lists most of the families that are eligible for membership in the Order of Founders and Patriots. It includes references to books or published articles on these families.

The best book in the Burton Collection to describe these patriotic and hereditary societies and to list the requirements necessary to join them is the *Hereditary Register of the United States of America.*

Listings for Patriotic and hereditary societies can be found in the Burton Main Catalog (No. 1).

## Surnames

The researcher should be aware that locating the origin and meaning of a surname can be very difficult. The majority of the surname books cover British surnames. The books that cover other surnames generally do not cover the East European countries very well. The researcher should bear in mind that not all the origins and meanings of surnames are known. Books on origins of surnames are not a major part of the Burton Collection's collecting scope. This subject is much better covered by the General Information Department in the Detroit Main Library. However, Burton does have some works in this field that are very good. The best overall surname book is Elsdon Smith's *Dictionary of American Family Names.* This work is arranged alphabetically and includes surnames from many European countries. For each name, the country of origin is given along with the meaning of the surname.

The best work on English surnames is *British Family Names.* This work was originally published in 1903 and was reprinted in 1968 by Gale

Research. It lists origins and meanings of English, Anglo-Saxon, Scandinavian, and Norman names.

There are two very good works that list origins and meanings of Irish surnames: Edward McLysaght's *Surnames of Ireland* and Patrick Kelly's *Irish Family Names.*

Scottish surnames are covered in *Surnames of Scotland: Their Origin, Meaning and History* by George F. Black. Again, origins and meanings of names are listed.

## Maps and Atlases

The maps in the Burton Collection cover the period 1500 to the present. They include maps of North America, New France, Canada, the Old Northwest, Michigan, and Detroit. Since Detroit was founded by the French in 1701, the emphasis on maps of New France in the early period is very strong. By the early nineteenth century, the maps emphasized Michigan Territory, created in 1805, and Detroit. The strongest area in the map collection is Michigan and, specifically, Detroit.

Generally speaking, maps do not include the names of property owners. This is very unfortunate for genealogists. Some maps – usually city maps – include buildings. This is especially helpful for those doing historic buildings research but of little help to genealogists. One of the few maps held by the Burton Collection that is helpful to locate property owners is John Farmer's Map of Wayne County, Michigan, 1855. This map is a complete map of the county including all of the townships and the property owners names in each township. The map does not include property owners in the city of Detroit. Maps can be found in the Atlas and Map Catalog (No. 5).

The atlases in the Burton Collection date back to 1474. The focus is the same as that of the maps. For the genealogist, the best type of atlas is the plat book. These cover one to three counties in each book and include a plat or drawing of each township in the county showing the property owners names. Burton's collection of New York, Ohio, Ontario, and Quebec atlases is very good. The best coverage again is for Michigan, especially the nineteenth century. Plat books began to be published in the mid 1860s and flourished into the first decade of the twentieth century. Probably the greatest impetus was the centennial of the Declaration of Independence in 1876. A review of plat books shows that many began to be published during this period. Many times there may be only one plat book of a county, and it was published in 1876. The Burton Collection has as many published plat books of Michigan counties as it has been able to locate. The most complete set are for counties around Detroit such as Wayne County. The Burton Collection holds plat books of Wayne County, Michigan for 1876, 1893, 1894, 1904, 1905, 1915, 1925, 1927, 1936. It also holds plat books for Oakland County, Michigan (neighboring County to Wayne) for 1872, 1894, 1896, 1908, 1921, 1927. Atlases can be found in the Atlases and Maps Catalog (No. 5).

Burton holds several atlases of Detroit. The earliest was published by Eugene Robinson in 1885. Rascher's Map of Detroit in three volumes was published in 1888. The Baist Real Estate Atlases of Detroit began in 1896, and the Burton Collection holds that year plus 1906, 1911, 1915, 1916, 1918, 1923, 1929, 1955. A companion to Baist is the Sanborn Insurance Maps which the Burton Collection holds for 1897-1953. Unfortunately, none of the Detroit atlases list property owners' names. They do list names of subdivisions and names of buildings and occasionally owners of buildings. Historic buildings researchers are the greatest users of these atlases because they include scale drawings of buildings on each plat of land.

## Land Records

Land records are generally kept in the county seat of each county in the United States. The earliest dates for each state vary. Generally, land records are not available in printed form; consequently, the Burton Collection holds very few land records in printed form. The exception is *Early Land Transfers, Detroit and Wayne County, Michigan 1703-1869*. This set will be discussed under state sources for Detroit and Michigan.

Some records concerning the very early years of the American nation are available. One source is the *American State Papers* which is held by the Burton Collection. This thirty-eight volume set includes the legislative and executive documents of the United States Congress from about 1789 to 1837. There are several sections to the set. They span foreign relations, Indian affairs, finance, commerce and navigation, military affairs, naval affairs, post office, public lands claims, and miscellaneous. The public lands section includes eight volumes and covers the period from 1790 to February 1837. One of the most important sets of records in the section on public lands is the private claims made for land in the United States. For instance, Detroit was founded by the French in 1701, came under British control in 1760, and finally became American in 1796. As a result of the American occupation, the local land holders had to establish their right to the land they had acquired under the French or British regimes. They did this by filing private claims with the United States government. The actions and granting of these private claims are found in the *American State Papers – Public Land* series.

A more specific source for private claims is the *Digested Summary of Alphabetical List of Private Claims which have been Presented to the House of Representatives from the 1st to the 31st Congress.* This three-volume set was originally published in 1853 and reprinted by the Genealogical Publishing Company in 1970. The alphabetical list gives the nature or object of a claim (such as correction, pension, confirmation of land title in a particular state, compensation for loss in war to government), how it was brought to the House, to which committee referred, date of report, nature of report, how disposed of by the House, how disposed of by the Senate, and the date of the act of Congress.

Another very good source is Clifford Neal Smith's *Federal Land Series.* This four-volume set is a calendar of land patents issued by the federal government to private individuals in states other than the original thirteen states. Much of the land was granted for service in the Revolutionary War and the War of 1812 based on military bounty land warrants.

The sources for the patents are archival records found in Washington, D.C., district land offices in various state archives, the legislative records of the United States House and Senate, and certain personal records of specific individuals such as Rufus Putnam and Richard Clough Anderson. The *Federal Land Series* covers the period 1788-1835 and is arranged by archival source with subject, tract, and name indexes.

## Newspapers

Burton holds some foreign newspapers such as the *London Chronicle* (1757-66). It also holds papers from cities such as Boston (*Columbian Centinel,* 1790-1818), Philadelphia (*Pennsylvania Gazette,* 1728-89), New York (*New York Herald,* 1859-68 and 1876-77), Washington, D.C. (*National Intelligencer,* 1812-48), and an anti-slavery newspaper from Windsor, Ontario (*Voice of the Fugitive,* 1851-5?).

The newspapers from Michigan cover a variety of cities such as Ann Arbor, Coldwater, Pontiac, and Warren. The Burton Collection carries very few long runs of newspapers from cities other than Detroit. Two exceptions are the *Sanilac Jeffersonian* (1858-98) and the *Pontiac Gazette* (1844-48 and 1850-1904). Newspapers rarely include actual genealogies, but they are excellent sources for obituaries of family members.

The best collection of newspapers covers Detroit. The earliest newspaper published in Detroit was the *Michigan Essay or Impartial Observer,* the first issue of which was published 31 August 1809; however, no other issue has been located. Later Detroit newspapers such as the

*Detroit Gazette* (1817-30), the *Detroit Daily Advertiser* (1836-62), and the *Detroit Journal* (1883-1921) are also held by the Burton Collection. Newspapers can be found in the Burton Main Catalog (No. 1).

The two longest running newspapers in Detroit are the *Detroit Free Press* and the *Detroit News*. The *Free Press* began publishing on 5 May 1831 and the *Detroit News* on 23 August 1873. The Burton Collection has a complete set of both newspapers in their original form from first publication through to 1960. The Burton Collection is attempting to preserve the originals, therefore patrons are referred to the microfilm copies in the General Information Department of the Detroit Public Library rather than use the original papers.

The Burton Collection has been clipping obituaries from the *Detroit News* and *Free Press* since the late 1930s. References to the obituaries can be found in the Detroit and Michigan Biography Index Catalog (No. 15).

Many newspapers including the *Detroit News* and *Free Press* have published vital records in the past. The publishing of vital records in the *Detroit News* and *Free Press* has been very irregular in the past and is not done at all today. The researcher must be aware that vital records are rarely required to be published in newspapers and that they are not published on the day the birth, death, or marriage occurred; therefore, the absence of one such date in a newspaper should not hastily be taken to mean that the event did not occur.

## Ethnic Groups

The Burton Collection has a wealth of material on ethnic groups. As with other subjects in the Burton Collection, the emphasis is on ethnic groups in Michigan and specifically Detroit. A review of the Burton catalogs reveals information on over fifty separate ethnic groups in Detroit. The entries include books, magazine articles, newspaper clippings, maps, photographs, and manuscripts. Entries are found in the Burton Main Catalog (No.1), the Local History File (No. 3), the Atlases and Maps Catalog (No.5), and the Picture File (No. 6). The researcher should look under the name of the ethnic group, then the place; for example: Germans in Detroit, Irish in Detroit, Jews in Detroit, Poles in Detroit, Ukrainians in Detroit.

There are very few books in the Burton Collection that cover several ethnic groups in one work. Generally, the works are about a particular ethnic group; however, there are two very good works that deal with more than one group. *Ethnic Groups in Detroit* by the Wayne University Department of Sociology and Anthropology is one of these. It was done as part of the work for Detroit's 250th anniversary in 1951. It covers forty-three ethnic groups from Albanians to Ukrainians. The work lists the basic history of the group and when the peak period of immigration occurred. It also records the area in Detroit where the group lived in the greatest concentration, and lists grocery stores, restaurants, special holidays, local funeral homes, and cemeteries where members of the group were buried. Although this source is obviously dated, it still provides the researcher with good basic information on Detroit's ethnic groups. Specific topics could be helpful to genealogists. Discussion of neighborhoods where specific groups settled may help genealogists place their own family or provide information on churches which were attended by a specific group.

The other good source on ethnic groups in Detroit is Lois Rankin's study *Detroit Nationality Groups.* Published in 1939, this is a study of twelve ethnic groups that includes Bulgarians, Macedonians, Finns, Greeks, Hungarians, Italians, Yugoslavs, Lithuanians, Poles, Rumanians, Russians, Syrians, and Ukrainians. Topics covered are approximate immigration dates, location of colonies (where groups lived in Detroit), occupations, religion, organizations, family life, social life, and community relations. The author's study has obvious limitations because it covers fewer ethnic groups than the Wayne study, but it is more detailed and specific for each group covered. For instance, under the Bulgarians and Macedonians, it mentions that "since unmarried men make up the greater part of the group, the girls usually marry early. Almost all who are of marriageable age were born in Europe." Although the information is dated, it tells the researcher that women of this ethnic group were married at an early age, which in many cases would have lead to the bearing of children well before a woman was twenty years old.

## Black Genealogy

In January 1977, "Roots" was shown on television. This dramatization of the life of a black family based on Alex Haley's book of the same name was the impetus for a major increase in use of the Burton Collection by genealogists. People of all races came to Burton in large numbers to trace their "roots." Specifically, many more blacks came to work on their genealogies. They found a good collection of materials that has continued to grow during the intervening decade.

Margaret Ward, the field worker responsible for collecting the papers of local black churches, individuals, and organizations, compiled an excellent list of sources entitled *Genealogical Sources for Afro-American Family Research in the Burton Historical Collection and the*

*Detroit Public Library.* This list contains over 100 sources and includes basic how-to books, free censuses and slave censuses, bibliographies of books on blacks, indexes of articles and books on blacks, city directories, vital records, and church records. Only selected sources will be discussed herein; it is recommended that the researcher consult the list in detail.

The following reports only a few of the several how-to books having to do with Ward's list. Charles Blockson's *Black Genealogy* and James Dent Walker's *Black Genealogy: How to Begin* are two of the older works, both having been published in 1977. Both give a good basic background on how to do black genealogy with suggestions on sources and solutions to problems. Kenn Stryker-Rodda's *Genealogical Research: Methods and Sources,* Volume II has a section entitled "Notes on Black Genealogical Research." This section includes an update on black genealogy from 1977 to 1983 and an excellent list of genealogical sources for Michigan, Alabama, Arkansas, Florida, Kentucky, Mississippi, Missouri, and Tennessee. The last source is Arlene Eakle and Johni Cerny's *The Source* that has a section entitled "Black Ancestral Research" which examines many problems in black genealogy and offers many suggested solutions with illustrations.

Census records specifically covering blacks begin with a *Census of the Slaves in New York in 1755.* This is followed by the *List of Free Black Heads of Families in the First Census of the United States, 1790* by Debra Newman. *Free Negro Heads of Families in the United States in 1830...* by Carter G. Woodson is a very good source for the tracing free blacks in the United States in 1830. *Free Black Heads of Households in the New York Census, 1790-1830* by Alice Eichholz and James M. Rose covers only New York state.

Burton holds microfilm copies of the original slave schedules of the United States census for 1850 and 1860. States held are Alabama, Arkansas, Delaware, Florida, Georgia, Kentucky, Louisiana, Maryland, Mississippi, Missouri, New Jersey, North Carolina, South Carolina, Tennessee, Texas, Virginia, and the District of Columbia. The lists give the name of the slave owner with the age, sex, and number of his slaves. There are no names given for the slaves.

There are three very good sources for information on specific blacks. First, *Blacks in Selected Newspapers Censuses, and Other Sources: An Index to Names and Subjects* indexes names and subjects about blacks. Second, *In Black and White: A Guide to Magazine Articles, Newspaper Articles and Books, Concerning more than 15,000 Black Individuals and Groups* locates individuals, cites careers, and lists sources for additional information. Third is the List of Pensioners on the Roll

January 1, 1883. This list includes everyone then receiving a pension from the United States and gives the name of each pensioner, cause for which each was pensioned, post office address, rate of pension per month, and date of original allowance. The list includes blacks who received pensions as a result of their service in the Civil War or earlier military service.

Burton's collection of war service records and related materials contains several very good sources that can be helpful to those working on black genealogy. *Index to Compiled Service Records of Volunteer Union Soldiers Who Served with U.S. Colored Troops* is an alphabetically arranged list of blacks who served for the North in the Civil War. The *Record of Service of Michigan's Volunteers in the Civil War 1861-1865, First Michigan Colored Infantry* lists blacks who served from Michigan giving their name, age upon enlistment, place of enlistment, a brief record of service including promotions, the discharge date and place, or place of death if the soldier died while in service. Peter Clark's *Black Brigade of Cincinnati* is a list of the black men from Cincinnati who comprised the Black Brigade of the Ohio Volunteers.

The collection of vital records includes several very good sources such as church records. Thomas Baldwin's *Vital Records of Cambridge, Massachusetts to the Year 1850* includes vital records pertaining to blacks. Another source is the *Register of Blacks in the Miami Valley: A Name Abstract, 1804-57*. From 1804 to 1857, Ohio law mandated that black people register their freedom papers with the Clerk of the County Common Pleas Court where they desired residency or employment. Other vital records include *Caldwell County North Carolina Marriages, 1841-66* including Cohabitation Records of 1866. *Records of Marriage of Henry County, Tennessee, 1881-1900* is an alphabetical index identifying Blacks by "col." *Winston County, Alabama Marriages, 1891-1900* includes marriages of blacks in one county of one of the states of the deep South.

A short list of some of the church records pertaining to blacks will give the researcher a good idea of the Burton Collection's material in that area: Parish Register of Bethel Africa Methodist Episcopal Church in Detroit, 1911-69; Marriage Register of Campbell Chapel A.M.E. Church, Chatham, Ontario, November 4, 1896-December 10, 1924; Black marriages in Register of Blacks, St. Landry Church, Opelousas, Louisiana, 1831-1840; Register of St. Francois des Natchitoches, 1800-1821 (including birth and death records of blacks); parish registers of St. Matthew's and St. Joseph's Episcopal Church, Detroit 1894-1975 (including confirmations, baptisms, marriages, and deaths); Second Baptist Church, Detroit, 1935-79 (including a register of marriages and deaths).

The works discussed above are only a few of the many sources for black genealogy in the Burton Collection. It is recommended that the researcher consult Margaret Ward's list, which is available from the Burton Collection, or the card catalogs under GENEALOGY – BLACK GENEALOGY.

## Heraldry and Nobility

Coats of arms were issued by the monarchs of Great Britain and Europe as a sign of favor for services rendered to the crown. They were used as a form of identification and to distinguish the nobility from other people. It is important to remember that there is not a coat of arms for every European or British name in existence.

Of books dealing with coats of arms, those devoted to British heraldry are the most informative in the Burton Collection. The *Encyclopedia of Heraldry* by Sir John Burke, published in 1851, is the most complete listing in one book covering coats of arms in England, Ireland, Scotland, and Wales. Unfortunately, this work has only written descriptions and is without pictures of the arms.

The genealogist will gain the most information from two other books by Burke and another book on British nobility. Burke's *Genealogical and Heraldic History of the Landed Gentry* and his *General Armory of England, Scotland, Ireland, and Wales* both include pictures of the coats of arms along with a lineage from the person to whom the arms were granted to the person who held them when the book was published. A more recent work is Arthur Fox-Davies' *Armorial Families*, published originally in the nineteenth century but republished in 1970. This work also has pictures of coats of arms, but more important, lineages.

The best book for European arms is the *Armorial General* by Johannes Rietstap (1926-50). This is actually two sets of books. The first set is a description, in French, of the coats of arms arranged alphabetically. The second is a six-volume set, also arranged alphabetically, of books with plates of each coat of arms. Various types of shadings, diagonal vertical, and horizontal lines, and dots are used to represent different colors in the arms.

The Burton Collection also holds books on coats of arms from certain other countries. Two on German arms are the *Hamburgische Wappenrolle* by Edward Lorenz-Meyer and Hugo Strohl's *Deutsche Wappenrolle*. Both have very good color plates of German coats of arms but neither includes lineages.

There are three very good works in the Burton Collection covering Polish arms. *Armorial de la Noblesses Polonaise Titree* by Szyman Konarski has pictures of coats of arms with descriptions in French in an alphabetical arrangement. *Ksiega Herbowa Radow Polskich, 1900* is an alphabetically arranged work with pictures of coats of arms and descriptions in Polish. The author has found many coats of arms in the Ksiega work that did not appear in the *Armorial General* or the *Armorial de la Noblesse Polonaise Titree.*

The last book on Polish coats of arms is *Herbarz Polski Kaspara Niesieckiego* by Kaspar Niescecki. This ten-volume set, published between 1839-46, is one of the largest works available on Polish coats of arms.

# Miscellaneous

### United Empire Loyalists

During the American Revolution, many people living in the colonies chose to remain loyal to the British monarch instead of supporting the colonists. These people were called Loyalists. When the British lost the war, these people were forced to leave their homes and go to territory still controlled by the British. Many went to Ontario, and they were called United Empire Loyalists. The Burton Collection has three very good works for the tracing of United Empire Loyalist connections. The first was published in 1885 by the United Empire Loyalist Centennial Committee. It is entitled *Centennial of the Settlement of Upper Canada by the United Empire Loyalists, 1784-1884.* It describes the celebration of the centennial in Adolphustown, Niagara, and Toronto. For the genealogist, there is a list of the United Empire Loyalists who went to Ontario via the Niagara River, giving the name, residence, descendants, and rank held by each loyalist.

A second work on United Empire Loyalists is Edward Chadwick's *Ontarian Families.* It covers fifty-seven families in Ontario along with their detailed genealogies. There is also an index of other families mentioned, including those who immigrated to Ontario at a later time.

The third book covering United Empire Loyalists is entitled *The Loyalists in Ontario* by William D. Reid. Loyalists who settled in Ontario after the Revolution were given land grants in recognition of their services and losses during the war. In addition, there was a provision for land grants for their sons and daughters. As these people petitioned for their land grants based on their parents' service, a notation was made of the authorization of each grant in the Council of Upper Canada. Mr. Reid extracted these authorizations and listed them under the name of the Loyalist father. In the case of daughters, the name of the husband is given, their place of residence, and the name of her father. Other information such as birth, marriage, and death dates, lot and concession numbers is sometimes given. This additional information was gathered from various sources by Mr. Reid and is discussed in the introduction of the book.

## Native American Genealogy Rolls

The Burton Collection holds two good sources for American Indian genealogy in Michigan. The originals for both are held by the National Archives in Washington, and the Burton Collection has microfilm copies.

The first is known as the *Durant Roll* because it was taken by Horace B. Durant. Its actual title is *The 1908 Census of the Chippewa Indians of Michigan*. It is a census roll of all persons and their descendants who were on the roll of the Ottawa and Chippewa Tribe of Indians in 1870 and living on 4 March 1907. It gives the name, relationship to the head of the family, age, sex, band within a tribe, and place of residence. Various facts are to be found in the section called "Remarks" such as "mother and father dead, separated from his wife, died on a particular date." The other source for Indian genealogy is Charles H. Dickson's *1910 Annuity Roll of Ottawas and Chippewas in Michigan*. It is really a census of Indians, including children, who received annuities from the United States due to treaty obligations. Everyone listed is named along with their relationship to the head of the family, age, sex, the amount of each check, the date of check or cash payment, signature of the person receiving the money, and the witness to the signature.

# 4
# Manuscripts

The manuscript collections of the Burton Historical Collection are composed of some 12 million items. They include personal papers, records of organizations, businesses, churches, and the governmental archives of Detroit and Wayne County, Michigan. The 2,360 collections of personal papers, organizations, businesses, and churches are well described in the *Guide to the Manuscripts in the Burton Historical Collection, Detroit Public Library* by Bernice Cox Sprenger. The *Guide* discusses the collections in detail so it is recommended that the researcher look at this work closely. There is a very good detailed index in the *Guide*. The archival records of Detroit and Wayne County, Michigan, are not listed in the *Guide*. It is hoped in the future that a supplement will be published listing the Detroit and Wayne County records. A review of the *Guide* for personal papers finds that there are forty-eight entries under individual or family names that specifically have references to genealogical information found in the papers of the individual or family. The information may include charts, genealogies, letters, or notes that yield genealogical information. This figure does not even include an additional fifty entries where "family letters" or correspondence with family members are mentioned.

Some listings for personal papers reveal that there is more material than just a single family genealogy. The Stephen Hull Papers actually include registers of marriages at Amesbury, Massachusetts (1800-12) and Raynham, Massachusetts (1812-22). The George Moore Papers contain marriages performed by Moore in Delaware and Maryland 1788-1810. The Charles I. Kanter Papers include the record book of the German-American Bank at Detroit, 1868-85. This record book may contain, aside from deposit information, birthplaces of depositors in Germany that can be very helpful to genealogists working on the Detroit German community.

The organizations recorded can be clubs, professional associations, charitable organizations, and other such groups. Papers on clubs and

THE GERMAN AMERICAN BANK, SAVINGS DEPARTMENT.

DEPOSITORS' SIGNATURES.

| DATE | BOOK NO | NAME | LOCALITY | OCCUPATION | NATIVITY | AGE | RESIDENCE | REMARKS |
|---|---|---|---|---|---|---|---|---|

11  Record of German-American Savings Bank found in the Charles Kanter Papers.

professional associations may contain lists of members which will help genealogists determine elements of their ancestors' personal lives. The papers of hereditary societies can also be very helpful to genealogical research. The Papers of the Sons of the American Revolution, Michigan Chapter, are one example. These include the original membership applications for entrance into the society along with lineages, and cover the period 1890 to 1973. Other examples are the New England Society of Detroit (1895-1916), the Society of Colonial Wars, Michigan (1899-1944), the Society of Mayflower Descendants, Detroit Chapter (1901-43).

Two other organizations' papers may be very helpful to genealogists. The papers of the Children's Aid Society (Detroit) cover the period 1860 to 1942, and the Children's Home of Detroit Papers cover the period 1836 to 1969. These organizations acted as orphan homes and adoption agencies for local families. Often they would take in children whose families could not take care of them for various reasons. Just as often the parents would return, at a later date, to retrieve their children. As a result, both societies maintained admission and surrender records showing when children were admitted and when they were surrendered to their parents. The records give the name of the child; the parents' names, if known; the child's residence; the birthplace, if known; and, in the Children's Home of Detroit Papers, a detailed description of the child's physical condition.

The papers of businesses generally have little information of use to genealogists. Occasionally, they may include employee records or payroll records that would indicate how long someone had worked for a company, but in most cases, this type of record is not part of a collection of manuscripts on a business.

Church records are excellent sources for genealogists. By the very nature of their purpose, birth, burial, confirmation, marriage, and membership records are kept by churches of all denominations. Some of the Detroit area church records held by the Burton Collection are those of the Central Methodist Church (1820-1970), Christ Church (1846-1906), Congregation Beth El (1850-1969), the First Presbyterian Church (1833-1963), Fort Street Presbyterian Church (1849-1962), Grosse Pointe Memorial Church (1860-1973), Redford Methodist Episcopal Church (1873-1924), Riverside Lutheran Church (1907-65), St. Paul's Cathedral (1820-1908), Tabernacle Baptist Church (1859-65), and Trumbull Avenue Presbyterian Church (1883-1924). The genealogist must be cautioned that the dates given above represent the earliest and latest item in each collection. Often the birth, burial, and marriage records do not cover all the dates in between.

The Burton Collection also holds records of some churches outside the Detroit area. These include the First Parish Church, Brookfield, Massachusetts (1817-57); Grace Episcopal Church, Mt. Clemens, Michigan (1868-1966); St. John's Church, Sandwich, Ontario (1807-57); St. Joseph, Michigan Catholic Mission (1720-72).

The manuscripts also contain three collections with family history materials on blacks. They are: Malcolm Dade (1831-1976), the Northcross Family (1899-1973), and the Pelham Family (1851-1948).

Two final manuscript sources should be mentioned. They are the records of the United States General Hospital (1864-65), which includes a register of sick and wounded soldiers taken to Harper, St. Mary's, and the Post Hospital at Detroit. The other source is Woodmere Cemetery (1871-1913) listing the burials of members of Congregation Beth El, the first synagogue in Detroit.

As was mentioned earlier, the *Guide to Manuscripts in the Burton Historical Collection, Detroit Public Library* does not contain descriptions of the archival records of the city of Detroit or Wayne County, Michigan. Although these governmental records do not contain vital records, certain collections can be useful to some genealogists.

The Tax Assessment Rolls of land in Wayne County, Michigan kept by the Wayne County Register of Deeds cover the years 1839-73. There are separate rolls for the ten wards in the city of Detroit and the townships outside Detroit but within Wayne County. The rolls give the name of the land owner, a description of the land, the section and township, acreage, value of each tract, and also state, county, township, and school tax. These tax assessment rolls can be especially helpful in determining when an ancestor came to Michigan and the length of time spent in a particular place.

The Wayne County Marriage Returns are an excellent source of information for genealogists with ancestors who were married in Wayne County. They cover the period 1818-88, although the majority cover the years 1860-77. These are the forms that ministers, judges, and justices of the peace filled out and sent to the county clerk who was required by law to record each birth, marriage, and death. The returns give the date of the marriage, the names of bride and groom, their color, residence, age, places of birth, and occupation. The returns were signed by the presiding minister, judge, or justice of the peace. Often the minister included the name of his church which could lead a genealogist to a church record of the marriage. In such records, this author was able to find the name of the small town in Germany where his paternal grandfather was born. A further search yielded the marriage return for his maternal grandfather, but the birthplace was only given as Bohemia. The point

288-H

[Dd.]

**288**

# RETURN OF A MARRIAGE.

• • •

TO THE CLERK OF THE COUNTY OF

*Wayne* _____ State of Michigan,

SIR:—On this _27th_ day of _August_ A. D. 187 8, the following named parties were joined in matrimony by me, at* _Detroit_ _____ _Mich._

<table>
<tr><td rowspan="6">**BRIDEGROOM.**</td><td>1. Full name of **Bridegroom**</td><td>*Frederick John Oldenburg*</td></tr>
<tr><td>2. Color of Bridegroom†</td><td>*White*</td></tr>
<tr><td>3. Residence at time of marriage</td><td>*Detroit Mich.*</td></tr>
<tr><td>4. Age at last birthday</td><td>*twenty four.*</td></tr>
<tr><td>5. Birthplace‡</td><td>*Wasdow Meklenburg Schwerin Germany*</td></tr>
<tr><td>6. Occupation</td><td>*Grocerist.*</td></tr>
<tr><td rowspan="6">**BRIDE.**</td><td>7. Full name of **Bride**</td><td>*Wilhelmine Sophia Friederike Schroeder*</td></tr>
<tr><td>8. Maiden name if a widow</td><td></td></tr>
<tr><td>9. Color of Bride†</td><td>*White*</td></tr>
<tr><td>10. Residence at time of marriage</td><td>*Detroit Mich.*</td></tr>
<tr><td>11. Age at last birthday</td><td>*nineteen*</td></tr>
<tr><td>12. Birthplace‡</td><td>*Kemmerich, Meklenburg Schwerin, Germany*</td></tr>
</table>

The witnesses to this marriage were:§

*Wilhelm Schröder* of *Detroit, Mich.* and

*Helmuth Oldenburg* " "

*C. H. Rohe*

*Pastor Ev. Luth St Pauls Church.*

**I hereby Certify,** That the foregoing is a true and correct transcript from my record of the marriage referred to.

*C. H. Rohe*

*Pastor*

Dated at *Detroit, Mich.* this *27th* day of *August* 187 8.

* State the township and county, or city.
† State whether WHITE, BLACK, MULATTO, INDIAN, WHITE and INDIAN, or other races.
‡ Give the State and Country.
§ Two witnesses required.
¶ Name and official title of magistrate or clergyman officiating, copied from his records.

12 Return of the marriage of Frederick Oldenburg and Wilhelmine Schroeder. From the Wayne County Marriage Returns.

here is that some ministers gave the town and country of birth on the marriage return while others listed only the country.

Another source for genealogists in the Detroit Archives is the papers of the Detroit House of Corrections. The Register of Prisoners covers the years 1861-1983, and there are indexes for all years. These records give the name of the prisoner, offense, nativity (birthplace), occupation, color, health on admission, weight on admission, and discharge. The important thing about the Register is that it may give a birthplace not found anywhere else or it may place an ancestor in Detroit at a particular time.

The last two items are not records of the city of Detroit or Wayne County, technically speaking, but are related and are particularly good for genealogical research on the early French in Detroit. The Detroit Notarial Records cover the years 1737-95 and are found in four typed volumes which have an index. These records were transcribed from the original records held by Wayne County. The French appointed royal notaries to record all transactions and legal business in Detroit. Legal transactions, certain business transactions, some marriages, and other similar events were recorded by the royal notaries. The Burton Collection holds a similar collection of typed transactions covering twenty-two indexed volumes for Montreal. The Montreal Notarial Records cover the years 1682-1822. These records are more business oriented and include indentures, business contracts, apprentices' and servants' contracts, and transactions related to the fur trade. Since Detroit was founded in 1701 by Cadillac, a Frenchman living in Montreal, these could be a useful source for Detroit genealogists with an early French line.

# 5
# *Sources by State*

This section is an attempt to record sources by state. It reflects those sources used regularly by the author or which have been referred to frequently by genealogists using the Burton Collection. It is not intended to be inclusive or exclusive in any way, rather, suggested sources for genealogists. It is recommended that genealogists check the Burton catalogs and P. William Filby's *American and British Genealogy and Heraldry* for further sources.

The Burton Collection holds the history of at least one county in every state with the exception of Alaska and Hawaii. The collection of county histories for each state generally includes histories of about half the counties in a state. The exceptions are the southern states of Florida, Alabama, Mississippi, Louisiana, Texas, Oklahoma, and Arkansas. Other states also having few county histories are South Dakota, North Dakota, Montana, Wyoming, and Nevada.

Most county histories were written in the latter half of the nineteenth century, the bulk of which were written after 1875. The centennial of the United States in 1876 seems to have spurred interest in history in general and local history in particular. Many county histories include sections on the townships and towns in the county and have a section of biographies of individuals prominent in the county when the county history was published. Many county histories are not indexed. If there is an index, it probably was done at a much later date by a local historian, genealogical society, or local historical society.

Generally speaking, the Burton Collection's list of town histories is very good. Massachusetts and Michigan have the most complete collections of town histories. The states of South Carolina, North Carolina, Florida, Alabama, Mississippi, Louisiana, Texas, Oklahoma, Arkansas, South Dakota, North Dakota, Montana, Wyoming, and Nevada have very few town histories.

Town histories usually have sections on education, churches, businesses, the founding of the city, cultural life, biographies of prominent persons, and other related sections. Like county histories, they usually are not indexed although they frequently have a list of the names of biographies that appear in the book.

The Burton Collection's holdings of vital records for the states are very scattered. One state, Massachusetts, has published vital records for most towns from the time the town was formed to 1850. Michigan's *Index Of Death Records* (1868-1914) and the *Index of Marriage Records* (1872-1921) cover the entire state. Most states in Burton have scattered vital records for counties or towns, and, usually, they cover the period before the state began recording vital records by law.

Most state sections in the Burton Collection have a magazine covering the history of the state. Burton's collection of historical magazines most often begins with the first issue and includes all issues up to the present day. These will sometimes have an index for each year.

There is a large collection of state genealogical magazines for various local and state genealogy societies. There is not a genealogical magazine for every state, and those that do exist often are not indexed. The genealogical magazines publish family histories, vital records, church records, land records, town records, court records, wills, probate records, Bible records, cemetery inscriptions, and genealogical queries.

The author has discussed the sources in an effort to present the different types of sources available in the state history sections in the Burton Collection. Not all of the of sources will be suggested under each state, and frequently, the only source for a state may be a historical or genealogical magazine.

When the coverage of a particular state is said to be poor, this should not be understood to reflect upon the Burton Collection. Many states, counties, and towns have very little published about them; therefore, the size of the collection in that area may be very small.

## New England

The best genealogical work on New England is James Savage's *Genealogical Dictionary of the First Settlers of New England.* This four-volume work includes three generations of settlers who came to New England before 1692. It is based on an earlier work by John Farmer, *A Genealogical Register of the First Settlers of New England* first published in 1829. Farmer's work included only specific groups of settlers such as governors, deputy governors, assistants, ministers, representatives in Massachusetts, Harvard graduates to 1662, members of the Ancient and Honorable Artillery Company, and freemen admitted to Massachusetts up to 1692. Savage claims to include all settlers who came before 1692.

Savage's work is arranged alphabetically by family name and lists birth, marriage, and death dates for three generations. It has a separate index of names mentioned in each settler's genealogy.

The *New England Historical and Genealogical Register,* published by the New England Historic Genealogical Society, is one of the best genealogical magazines available in this country. It first appeared in 1847, and the Burton Collection has a complete set of issues published. There is an index of persons, places, and subjects covering the years 1847-97 and an index of subjects only for the years 1897-1958. The *Register* has been indexed annually since 1958.

### Maine

There are county histories for most of the counties in Maine and a good number of town histories.

The *Maine Historical Quarterly* is the best magazine for the general history of Maine. Burton has all issues from 1962 to the present. There is an index in each volume.

The *Maine Genealogical Inquirer* is the only genealogical magazine the Burton Collection holds for Maine with issues for 1969-75. There is an index in each volume.

### New Hampshire

The county and town histories of New Hampshire are complete.

The *Provincial Papers, Documents and Records relating to the Province of New Hampshire* is a very good source for genealogical information. This forty-volume work covers the period 1636-1860 and includes letters, town charters, probate records, biographies, and other documents helpful to genealogists. Volumes 14-17 contain the rolls and documents relating to soldiers in the Revolutionary War. It lists such information as name, rank, residence, name of regiment, and how many rations were received.

Each volume of the *Provincial Papers* is separately indexed.

### Vermont

There are histories of most of the counties for Vermont and the number of town histories is very good.

*The Rolls of the Soldiers in the Revolutionary War 1775-83* published by the state of Vermont in 1904 is a very complete list of men from Vermont who fought in the Revolution. It is made up of payrolls but also includes militia payrolls and muster rolls. It is arranged chronologically with an alphabetical index of persons and towns.

**Massachusetts**

The county histories of Massachusetts are fairly complete. There are town histories for all but the very small towns in the state. This group is the most complete of the town histories of any state in the Burton Collection.

*Massachusetts Soldiers and Sailors of the Revolutionary War,* published by the state, is the most comprehensive and detailed state list of persons who served during the Revolution in the Burton Collection. This twenty-seven-volume work is arranged alphabetically and provides the name, place of enlistment, rank, service record, including the names of regiments in which served, discharge information, and an interesting category labeled "stature." An example will suffice: "Israel Blackington, stature 5 feet 6 inches, residence Cambridge." It is rare for a genealogist to locate the height of an ancestor, especially one from the Revolutionary period!

Another good source for genealogical information is the *Essex Institute Historical Collections* published by the Essex Institute in Salem, Massachusetts. The Burton Collection has all the issues of this annual publication from 1859 to the present. It includes genealogies, church records, town records, vital records, court records of Essex County, wills of Essex County, witchcraft documents and trials, and also war diaries of the men who fought in the French and Indian War and the Revolution. There is an index for the *Collections* for the years 1859-1969.

Massachusetts is one of the few states that has an extensive vital records account in the Burton Collection. There are vital records for almost every town from its earliest date to 1850. They were published by the New England Historic Genealogical Society and the Essex Institute.

The *Mayflower Descendant* is one of the better sources for information on families who came to Massachusetts on the *Mayflower.* This magazine was published from 1899 to 1937 by the Massachusetts Society of Mayflower Descendants and contains vital records, wills, probate records, deeds, church records, genealogies and other genealogical topics. There is a complete index for all persons mentioned from 1899-1937, and there are indexes of subjects and places in each volume.

Another source for tracing *Mayflower* descendants is the *Mayflower Index* by William Alexander McAuslan. This work is an index to approved lineages on file with the General Society of Mayflower Descendants prior to February 1931. It gives the name, number, spouses's name, and parents' names for each name that occurs in the first four generations. This two-volume set was revised in 1960 by Lewis E. Neff, and a third volume was added with new names up to 1 January 1960.

Early Massachusetts records such as the *Records of the Town of Plymouth* are also good for those working in Massachusetts genealogy. This three-volume set covers 1636-1783 and includes land transactions, laws, town meeting reports, boundaries, cattle marks, and other genealogical information. There is an alphabetical index in each volume.

One of the better sources for early Massachusetts and New England is *Mayflower Families through Five Generations.* Published by the General Society of Mayflower Descendants in Plymouth, Massachusetts, this work, of which three volumes have been published, selects persons who came on the *Mayflower* and traces their ancestry for five generations from the Plymouth landing in 1620. Within the three volumes there are seven separate families recorded, including birth, marriage, and death dates for each generation with sources for the information. There is an index for all names in each work.

### Rhode Island

The county histories for Rhode Island are complete. The town histories are extensive, that for Providence being detailed, with fairly good coverage for smaller towns.

A major source for Rhode Island research is John Osborne Austin's *Genealogical Dictionary of Rhode Island.* It comprises three generations of settlers who came to Rhode Island before 1690. Very well documented, this volume should be checked by anyone working on Rhode Island genealogy.

The *Vital Records of Rhode Island 1636-1850* by James N. Arnold is extensive, covering twenty-one volumes. They were compiled from town records and newspaper lists and include the Revolutionary War Rolls and pensions in volume 12. There is an index in each volume.

An even more detailed work for Providence is the *Alphabetical Index of the Births, Marriages, and Deaths Recorded in Providence from 1636.* This work covers the years 1636-1935 and is found in twenty-five volumes, each volume alphabetically arranged. The volume and page of the city record are given beneath the name of each individual.

### Connecticut

Burton holds an excellent collection of county and town histories for the entire state of Connecticut.

The *Record of Service of Men in the War of the Revolution, War of 1812, Mexican War* gives the name of each man, enlistment date, and rank for the Revolutionary veterans, including naval and militia units. There is a separate index for Revolutionary veterans. Under the War of

1812, the name, rank, place of service, commander, and period of service are given.

Connecticut is another state with a very good collection of vital records. Lucius Barnes Barbour created the *Barbour Collection of Connecticut Vital Records* on cards in the Connecticut State Library. These records have been microfilmed and are made up of two parts. The first part is an alphabetical listing by name with a card for each individual. These are found on eighty-one reels of microfilm. The other part is an alphabetical listing of all the town records found on seventeen reels of microfilm. The best way to use the records is to look up a person on the individual list, and their card will refer you to the records by town names.

Another Connecticut item is Donald L. Jacobus's *History and Genealogy of the Families of Old Fairfield*. This three-volume work in five books covers genealogies alphabetically, beginning with the first person to come to Fairfield, and it traces their line to 1700 or 1720 – some even later. It is based on local genealogies, vital records, manuscripts of the Fairfield Historical Society, probate records, gravestone inscriptions, and church records. There is an index in each volume.

Jacobus wrote another item that is useful to genealogists working on Connecticut. That is *Families of Ancient New Haven*. This eight-volume work includes the earliest person in the family to come to New Haven down to the heads of families in the 1790 census and includes the generation born between 1790 and 1800. The sources for the information are vital records, church registers, land records, probate records, town records, family or private records, and cemetery inscriptions. There is a separate index for those names not included in the main genealogies of the work.

This work was originally entitled the *New Haven Genealogical Magazine* from 1922-31 and is actually the first eight volumes of *The American Genealogist*.

### New York

The counties of New York are well represented through county histories. There are many town histories with the most extensive information to be found being that on Albany, Buffalo, and New York City. The *New York Genealogical and Biographical Record* is one of the best genealogical magazines for New York. It began in 1870, and the Burton Collection has every issue from the first to the present. There is a name index in each volume and a separate surname index for the years 1870-1909. There is a master subject index for 1870-1982.

Another good genealogical magazine is *Tree Talks* published by the Central New York Genealogical Society. Burton has the issues from its inception in 1961 to the present. *Tree Talks* has an index in each volume. As mentioned, there are many histories on the city of New York, but there are few vital records. The *New York Evening Post* deaths from 1801-35 are published as are the marriages from 1801-79. Both are arranged by date with indexes in each volume.

## Pennsylvania

There are county histories for most counties in Pennsylvania, but the coverage on towns is not as good. An exception is Philadelphia for which coverage is excellent and in depth.

*The Pennsylvania Archives, 1874-1935* is the best general work on Pennsylvania. It covers the state from the earliest colonial times to the nineteenth century. It includes all types of documents on the state and the same type of material as is published in genealogy magazines. There are nine separate series in the set. Occasionally, the index for one series will be found in the following series. Volumes 5-8 of Series Five contain *Pennsylvania in the War of Revolution; with Associated Battalions and Militia, 1775-1783.*

The Pennsylvania German Society *Proceedings* and *Addresses,* covering the years 1891-1965, is one of the best sources for Pennsylvania German genealogy. These annual proceedings include biographies of Pennsylvania Germans, church records, and addresses on various subjects. Volumes 42-44 (1934 ) by Ralph Strassburger are entitled *Pennsylvania German Pioneers.* This is a publication of the original lists of arrivals in the port of Philadelphia from 1727 to 1808, giving the names of the passengers, the ship and date of arrival. There is an index in volume 44. This book was republished in 1980 as *Pennsylvania German Pioneers* by Ralph B. Strassburger and William J. Hinke.

Early Pennsylvania naturalizations are recorded in Montague S. Guiseppi's *Naturalization of Foreign Protestants in America and the West Indian Colonies,* but *Philadelphia Naturalization Records*, edited by P. William Filby, is a more inclusive source for naturalizations in Pennsylvania. It is an index to records of aliens, declarations of intentions and/or oaths of allegiance from 1789 to 1880. It covers several different courts in Philadelphia and gives the name of the individual, country of former allegiance, court, and the date of the declaration of intention or oath of allegiance. The work is arranged alphabetically.

## New Jersey

There are histories of most counties in New Jersey and histories for the larger towns.

The *New Jersey Archives* is similar to the set for Pennsylvania and just as good for genealogists. There are two series which were published by the New Jersey Historical Society between 1880 and 1949. They publish *Documents Relating to The Colonial History of New Jersey* and, abstracts of wills and newspaper extracts from American newspapers, especially for the period 1776-82.

The best journal for the state is the *Genealogical Magazine of New Jersey* published by the Genealogical Society of New Jersey. The Burton Collection has issues from 1925 to the present. There is a name index for the period 1925-75 written by Kenn Stryker-Rodda, one of the foremost genealogists of our day.

## Delaware

The collection of material on Delaware has few county histories and town histories. A good history of the state is Thomas J. Scharf's *History of Delaware 1609-1888*. This two-volume work covers the history of the state very well. Its three-volume index was published in 1976 by the Historical Society of Delaware.

The *Delaware Archives* published by the Public Archives Commission of Delaware is similar to the *Pennsylvania Archives* and the *New Jersey Archives*. The five volumes include documents relating to the history of Delaware from *King George's War (1744-48)* to *The Delaware Militia of 1827*. There is an index for the set.

## Maryland

The number of county histories on Maryland is not large but adequate. There are few town histories.

The *Maryland Genealogical Society Bulletin*, published by the society, is a very good source for genealogical information on Maryland. The Burton Collection has a complete set of issues from its inception in 1960 to the present. Unfortunately, there is no index.

Another genealogical magazine on Maryland is *Western Maryland Genealogy* published by Donna Valley Russell. It began in 1985, and the Burton Collection has all of the issues from 1985 to the present. This magazine covers the western counties of Frederick, Washington, Allegeny, Montgomery, Carroll, and Garrett.

The *Maryland and Delaware Genealogist* is published by Raymond B. Clark, Jr., and is dedicated to publishing source material on Maryland

and Delaware. The Burton Collection has a complete set of the publication from 1959 to the present. There is an index for each year.

A very good source for wills in Maryland is Jane Baldwin Cotton's *Maryland Calendar of Wills 1636-1743*. This eight-volume work is composed of abstracts of wills from the Prerogative Court of the Province. The bequests are covered in good detail under each will, and the work is arranged chronologically. There is an index in each volume.

A good source for research on early Maryland is the *Archives of Maryland*. Published by the Maryland Historical Society, this seventy-two volume set includes the proceedings and acts of the general assembly, proceedings of the provincial court, early proceedings of the county courts, muster rolls, and other records of the service of Maryland troops in the Revolution. There is an index in each volume.

Another source of information on Maryland is the *Indexes to Testamentary Proceedings* by Annie Walker Burns. This multivolume work, published between 1936 and 1939, includes probates of wills and letters of the administration of estates from 1657 to 1768. It is arranged alphabetically and gives the name of the person, liber, folio, year, and county. It is important for the researcher to know that this is only an index which tells where to find the original. It does not give the complete will or letter of administration itself.

### District of Columbia

The collection of materials on the District of Columbia is not very large. A majority of the books deal with the history of the District. There is no genealogical magazine. There is, however, a historical magazine entitled *Records of the Columbia Historical Society* that covers the years 1894-1952, and it has a full index.

## Southern States

### West Virginia

There are a good number of West Virginia county histories but few town histories in the Burton Collection. For the period before 1863, West Virginia records are found under Virginia.

The *SIMS Index to Land Grants in West Virginia*, prepared by Edgar Barr Sims and published by the state of West Virginia in 1952, is the best source for early land holdings in West Virginia. This is an alphabetical list of land grants made by Lord Fairfax prior to creation of Virginia under its first constitution. The work is based on the original volume in the State Auditor's Office and gives the name of the grantee, acreage, a local description, the year, book, and page.

### Virginia

The Burton Collection has a good collection of county histories for Virginia and a fairly good collection of town histories.

The *Virginia Historical Index* by Earl G. Swem, published in 1934, is probably the best source of genealogical information for Virginia. This two-volume work, arranged alphabetically, indexes every name and place in five historical magazines and two multivolume works. The works indexed are the *Virginia Magazine* for 1893-1930; *William and Mary Quarterly* (1892-1930); *Tyler's Quarterly* (1919-1929); *Virginia Historical Register* (1848-1853); *Lower Norfolk County, Virginia Antiquary* (1895-1906); *Henings Statutes at Large* (1619-1792); *Calendar of Virginia State Papers* (1652-1869).

The *Virginia Genealogist,* published since its inception in 1957 by John F. Dorman, is one of the best genealogical magazines on Virginia. Dorman says in the introduction to Volume 1 (1957) that he began the magazine to publish source materials and accounts of Old Dominion families because the *William and Mary Quarterly* did not publish family records. Each volume is indexed, and the Burton Collection has a complete set of all issues of this magazine.

### North Carolina

There are a good number of county histories for North Carolina, but as with many southern states, few town histories. The *North Carolina Genealogical Society Journal* published by the Society provides good coverage on this state. The Burton Collection has a complete set of the magazine from its inception in 1975 to the present. The magazine has an index in each volume.

North Carolina is one of the few Confederate states that has published a list of men who fought in the Civil War. *North Carolina Troops 1861-1865* is being published by the State Department of Archives and History. Envisioned as a twelve-volume work when begun in 1966, eight volumes have been published thus far. Volume 1 covers the artillery, volume 2 the cavalry, and volume 3-8 the infantry. The remaining volumes (9-12) will complete the infantry. The volumes are arranged by regiment, giving the name of each individual, their service record, and enlistment and discharge dates. There is an index in each volume.

## South Carolina

As with North Carolina, there are a good number of county histories but few town histories for South Carolina.

The best genealogical magazine for South Carolina is the *South Carolina Historical and Genealogical Magazine.* The articles in this journal mix history and genealogy. Until 1953, it was entitled the *South Carolina Historical Magazine.* The Burton Collection holds issues from volume one (1900) to the present. There is a two-volume index for 1900-70.

## Georgia

There are a good number of county histories for Georgia but few town histories.

The *Georgia Genealogical Magazine,* which began in 1961, publishes source material on Georgia. The Burton Collection has all issues published. There is an index in each volume.

Many southern states have very few county and town histories in the Burton Collection. The following states are in that category. Genealogical magazines for those states are listed below.

## Florida

*Florida Genealogist* (1981 to the present). There is an index in each volume.

## Alabama

*Alabama Genealogical Register* (1959-68). Each volume includes an index.

## Mississippi

*Mississippi Genealogical Exchange* (1955 to the present). Each volume includes an index.

## Louisiana

*Louisiana Genealogical Register* (1954 to the present). Each volume includes an index.

*New Orleans Genesis* (1962 to the present). There is no index.

## Texas

*Stirpes* (1961 to the present). Each volume includes an index.

*Heart of Texas Records,* which began as the *Central Texas Genealogical Society Quarterly* (1958 to the present). Each volume includes an index.

## Arkansas

*Arkansas Family Historian* (1962 to the present). Each volume includes an index.

## Tennessee

The Burton Collection has a very good collection of county histories for Tennessee. *Goodspeed's History of the Counties of Tennessee* reprints the county histories originally published in 1886 and 1887. There are forty-two counties covered, but unfortunately, these are not indexed.

Tennessee is another southern state that has published a list of men who served in the Civil War. *Tennesseans in the Civil War,* published in 1964 and 1965 by the Tennessee Civil War Centennial Commission, is a two-part work covering the military history of Confederate and Union units with available rosters of personnel. Part 1 is a history of each unit listing battle engagements, officers for each unit, and enlistment dates. There is an index of soldiers, regiments, and companies mentioned. Part 2 contains two separate alphabetical lists of the men who fought for the Confederacy and the Union, giving each man's name, company, regiment or unit.

## Kentucky

There are a good number of county histories for Kentucky. but again, few town histories.

Kentucky has two very good historical magazines that may be of help to genealogists. The *Filson Club History Quarterly* began publishing in 1926 and the Burton Collection has issues from that date to the present. There is an index in each volume. The other magazine is the *Register of the Kentucky State Historical Society.* The Burton Collection has complete issues of this publication from 1917 to the present along with scattered earlier issues. There is a general index, from 1903-45, and there are indexes in each volume also.

One of the best genealogical magazines for Kentucky is the *Kentucky Genealogist.* Published by Martha Miller from 1959 to 1983, it is presently published by James Bentley. The Burton Collection has issues from its inception in 1959 to the present. There is an index in each volume.

## The Great Lakes and Midwest States

The states of the Midwest will be covered separately, but there is one very good genealogical magazine that should be mentioned. The *Old Northwest Genealogical Quarterly* was published from 1898 to 1912. It has an excellent coverage of the genealogy of this area of the country. There is an index for each volume.

The Burton Collection has an excellent collection of materials on the history of the Great Lakes. There are histories of the Lakes, lists of shipping companies, ships, shipwrecks, and magazines with articles about the Great Lakes and shipping on the Lakes.

John B. Mansfield's *History of the Great Lakes* is probably the best general history of the Lakes. The first volume of this work includes histories of the Lakes, shipbuilding company histories, stories of the building of Great Lakes ships and shipwrecks, and a list including the name of each ship, type, tonnage, date built, where built, if still in commission as of the printing of this book in 1899 or whether it had sunk and where with the date of the shipwreck. Volume 2 includes biographies of company officers and prominent captains who sailed the Lakes.

Frequently, genealogists ask for lists of captains who have sailed on the Great Lakes because someone in their family had been a ship's captain. There is one very good list of early captains on the Lakes: the *Marine Directory of the Great Lakes* published in 1888. It has a section listing all the ships operating on the Lakes when the book was published. The captains are listed by name, their place of residence, and vessel.

There are two very good magazines that should be checked for information by genealogists working on the Great Lakes. The first is *Inland Seas*. The Burton Collection has a complete collection from 1945 to the present. There are biographies of men who have sailed the Lakes, company histories, ship histories, and stories of shipwrecks. There is an index in each volume.

The other magazine on the Great Lakes is *Telescope*. It first appeared in 1952, and the Burton Collection's files are complete to the present. Its articles are similar to those in *Inland Seas,* and it contains many photographs of ships that have sailed the Lakes. There is an index in each volume.

### Ohio

The Burton Collection has county histories for almost all counties in Ohio. The town histories are not extensive, though there are histories of Cincinnati, Cleveland, Columbus, Springfield, and Toledo.

*Ohio Records and Pioneer Families,* published by the Ohio Genealogical Society, is one of the best genealogical magazines on the state. It began in 1960, and the Burton Collection has all the issues from that date to the present. There is an index in each volume.

### Indiana

There are county histories for almost all the Indiana counties. Town histories are much fewer in number.

The *Hoosier Genealogist* by the Genealogical Section of the Indiana Historical Society is one of the best genealogical magazines dealing with Indiana. Its first issue appeared in 1961, and the Burton Collection has all issues since that date. There is an index in each volume.

### Illinois

The Illinois county histories are as extensive as those of Ohio and Indiana. The Burton Collection holds a good collection of Chicago histories, but there are few other town histories available.

The *Illiana Genealogist*, published by the Illiana Genealogical and Historical Society, is one of the Illinois genealogical magazines. The Burton Collection has issues from 1965 to the present. Unfortunately, this magazine does not have an index.

### Michigan

There are county histories for virtually all counties in Michigan. There are many town histories with the best coverage being that devoted to Detroit. The Burton Collection specializes in the history of Detroit and Michigan; therefore, they have something on almost any aspect of the history of that city and state.

There are three very good magazines that genealogists should check when working on Michigan genealogy. *Michigan History* is the oldest ongoing magazine dealing with the history of Michigan. The Burton Collection has issues from its first issue in 1917 to the present. There is an index for volumes 1-25, 26-46, and 47-57. There is an index in each volume from 58 to the present.

The *Flint Genealogical Quarterly* published by the Flint Genealogical Society was published from 1959-83 and the Burton Collection has all the issues for those years. It has a surname index in each volume.

Another genealogical magazine is *Michigan Heritage* published by the Kalamazoo Valley Genealogical Society from 1959-73. This magazine was especially good for genealogical research concerned with the west side of the state of Michigan. *Michigan Heritage* has an index in each volume and the Burton Collection holds all of the issues of this magazine.

The Burton Collection also holds a good collection of city directories for at least two of the major cities in the state outside Detroit. The Flint city directories include 1885 and scattered years from 1922-69. The Grand Rapids city directories cover the years 1868-54. The directories are scattered for the years 1868-87 and 1923-54 but are complete. from 1888-1922.

Another good research source for Michigan is its telephone directories. The Burton Collection has an extensive collection covering virtually every town in the state. The most complete set is for Detroit, beginning with 1878, and it will be discussed later. The telephone books for other towns generally begin about 1939 and run to the present. The Burton Collection has complete collections of the telephone books for Flint, Grand Rapids, Kalamazoo, and Lansing. The collections for the smaller towns are not as complete and may begin later than 1939.

Newspapers can be very good sources for genealogical information especially as regards obituaries. The Burton Collection has a complete file of the *Detroit Free Press* (1831 to the present) and the *Detroit News* (1873 to the present). Its collection of newspapers for other Michigan cities is not as extensive. The Burton Collection has the *Cheboygan Democrat* (1888-98), *Der Arme Teufel,* a German newspaper (1885-97), the *Lansing Journal* (1872-82), the *Pontiac Daily Press* (1934-38; not all issues), the *Pontiac Gazette* (1844-48 and 1850-1904; not all issues), and the *Sanilac Jeffersonian* (1858-98).

Michigan's list of Civil War soldiers, *Record of Service of Michigan Volunteers in the Civil War, 1861-1865,* is one of the most complete of all the states. The forty-six-volume set includes one volume on each regiment. Each volume is arranged alphabetically. For each individual the service record, enlistment, and discharge dates are given. There is one index for the entire set.

Frances Loomis's *Michigan Biography Index* was published by the Detroit Public Library in 1946. It is an index of biographical sketches in printed books that deal exclusively with Michigan. County histories, state histories, city histories, and biographical works are typical items indexed. It is arranged alphabetically and gives the name, year of birth, source, and page number for biographical sketches in over 200 books.

An important source for early Michigan records is the *Historical Collections* of the Michigan Pioneer and Historical Society. This forty-volume set was published from 1877 to 1929. It contains extensive genealogical information in the form of memoirs, reminiscences, biographies, county records, and other historical records for genealogists. It is really a gold mine for genealogists. There is a separate two-volume genealogical index to the complete set and a separate index of subjects, persons, and places for volumes 1-15 and 16-30. Each volume from 31-40 has a separate index for persons, places, and subjects.

Another source for records concerning Michigan before it became a state is Clarence Carter's *Territorial Papers of the United States.* This multivolume set presents material on several states, which includes documents that were written during a state's territorial period. The volumes on the *Northwest Territory, 1787-1805* and *Michigan Territory, 1805-37* are excellent sources for early genealogical records for Michigan.

The Michigan Daughters of the American Revolution have published a work that is very helpful to Michigan genealogists. *DAR Bible and Pioneer Records* covers thirty-seven volumes and includes. bible, genealogical, family, and vital records. There is a three-volume index to the complete set.

Another source for Michigan is the *Index to Deaths, 1867-1914* and the *Index to Marriages, 1872-1921.* Both give the name of the individual and the volume and page of the record in the Michigan Board of Health Department of Vital Statistics located in Lansing, Michigan.

### Detroit and Wayne County, Michigan

The available records of Detroit and Wayne County, Michigan, are quite extensive. The Louisa St. Clair Chapter of the National Society of the Daughters of the American Revolution in conjunction with the Works Progress Administration prepared a transcription of a series of excellent works for genealogists. The *Birth Records from the Archives of Wayne County* and the *Death Records of the Detroit Board of Health* both cover the period 1835-70. The *Birth Records* are arranged alphabetically in four volumes. The *Death Records* are found in four volumes and are. listed by name of cemetery, i.e., Catholic cemetery, and Mount Elliott cemetery. The fifth volume is an alphabetical index to the set.

The Louisa St. Clair chapter has also transcribed the *Death Records of Mount Elliott Cemetery, 1841-70,* and *Death Records of Elmwood Cemetery, 1837-70,* and the *Vital Records from the Detroit Free Press 1831-68.* Mount Elliott was the Roman Catholic cemetery and Elmwood was the Protestant cemetery in Detroit. The two-volume Mount Elliott records are arranged according to the sections of the cemetery, giving the name, parish, date of death, and age of the individual. There is an alphabetical index in Volume 2. The four-volume Elmwood records are arranged by plot number and give the name, birthplace, place of death, date of death, and age of the individual. There is an alphabetical index in volume 4. The *Free Press* records include births, marriages, and deaths arranged alphabetically under those headings in each year. There is an alphabetical index with each volume.

Another set of works by the DAR Louisa St. Clair chapter are *Marriage Records from the Archives of Wayne County, 1835-1870* arranged alphabetically by groom with a separate brides index, and *Early Land Transfers, Detroit and Wayne County, Michigan, 1703-1869*. This fifty-three volume set covers land transfers throughout Detroit and Wayne County. Each volume covers a different set of years and is arranged alphabetically. There is a four-volume general index for the complete set. *Early Land Transfers* gives names of the purchaser and seller, date, a description of the land, witnesses, date recorded, and volume and page of the original volume in which a record was made.

Another work by the Louisa St. Clair Chapter of the DAR is the *Probate Records of Wayne County, Michigan*. This five-volume set. is arranged chronologically from the earliest probate record in 1797 to 1870. Abstracts of the records are given listing the name of the individual, place, filing date, petitioner, guardian if one was appointed, size of estate, and beneficiaries. There is an index in each volume.

The Burton Collection has a complete set of Detroit city directories for the years:

| | |
|---|---|
| 1837 | 1963 east side |
| 1845 | 1964 east and west side |
| 1846 | 1965 west side |
| 1850-1941 | 1967 east side |
| 1953 west side | 1968 east and west side |
| 1954 east side | 1969 west side |
| 1956 west side | 1970 east and west side |
| 1957 east side | 1973 west side |
| 1958 west side | 1974 east side |

There were no city directories published for the years 1942-52.

The Burton Collection also has Detroit telephone directories for 1878, 1879, 1882, 1883, 1886, 1887, 1890, and from 1892 to the present.

The city directories give the name of each person, the occupation, and address. They are one of the best sources to determine whether a person lived in the city in a particular year. They are also a good source for people with the same last name and a source for determining the ward boundaries for the United States censuses for 1860, 1870, and 1880. The city directories in the period covering approximately 1890-

1910 listed deaths and the names of those who left the city in the previous year.

The best genealogical magazine for Michigan is the *Detroit Society for Genealogical Research Magazine.* Burton has issues from 1937 when it began to the present. There are five cumulative indexes for the magazine for the years 1937 to 1967, and there is an index in each volume since then.

Of special interest to those with French-Canadian ancestors is *Genealogy of French Families of the Detroit River Region, 1701-1911* by Christian Denissen, which was published in 1976 by the Detroit Society for Genealogical Research. This two-volume set updated in 1987 to the year 1937 is the best work on the early French in Detroit. It alphabetically lists families of the founders and earliest settlers of Detroit. Each genealogy is given completely from the earliest family member found, sometimes in France, to 1936. There is an index for names that do not have a separate family line in the work. Any genealogist working on the early French in Detroit must use this work.

The Burton Collection includes several detailed parish registers for early Catholic churches in Detroit as well as in other parts of Michigan. The largest of these registers is the Registre de St. Anne Church. Founded in 1701, this Roman Catholic church is the oldest church in Detroit. The register, in French, is actually a handwritten transcription of the original now held by the Archdiocese of Detroit. It covers the period 1704-1848 and consists of seven volumes covering baptisms, marriages, and burials. There is a separate three-volume alphabetical index for the set. Since St. Anne's was the only church in Detroit until the beginning of the nineteenth century, it includes burials, marriages, and baptisms of many people who were not Catholics, simply because the register was the only religious means through which these activities might be recorded.

Another church register related to St. Anne's is the Registre des Paroisses Exterieures. This register covers the years 1810-33 and includes the Catholic parishes exterior or out of the immediate area of St. Anne's but under its jurisdiction for the purpose of the record keeping of baptisms, marriages, and burials. The register is also a handwritten transcription in French with its own index. The parishes covered are L'Anse Creuse, Arbre Croche, Auxs pieds rapides, (Foot of the Rapids), Boie Verte (Green Bay), Mackinac, Prairie du Chien, Riviere aux Huron (Clinton River), Riviere St. Clair, Salt River, and Saulte Sainte Marie.

Volumes 18 and 19 of the *Collections* of the State Historical Society of Wisconsin contain the registers of baptisms, marriages, and burials of the Catholic parish at Mackinac for the period 1695-1821. These registers are written in English. Volume 18 has the register of marriages (1725-1821), and volume 19 has baptisms and burials (1695-1821). Both volumes have their own indexes.

The last of the Catholic parish registers is the Registre de la Pariosse de l' Assumption (31 August 1752-31 December 1824). This covers Assumption Parish located in Sandwich–present day Windsor, Ontario, across the Detroit River from Detroit. This is also in French with a handwritten transcription. The three-volume work includes baptisms, marriages, and burials, and there is a separate one-volume index for the set.

The Archdiocese of Detroit has deposited microfilm copies of the registers of seventy-three Roman Catholic parishes in and around Detroit. These registers began as early as 1701 with St. Anne's Church and include all churches for which the Archdiocese holds records. The records include baptisms, confirmations, marriages, and deaths from the first records made for each church until 1900. The records must be searched in person, and a form must be submitted to the Burton Collection before they may be used. These records are especially good for ethnic groups that emigrated to the Detroit area in the last half of the nineteenth century such as the Polish and eastern European ethnic groups.

## Great Plains and Far West

The books on the Great Plains and the Far West are not used as regularly as the books on the other states. As a result, recommendations on specific sources are more difficult. Generally speaking, the county histories are good for Wisconsin, Minnesota, Iowa, Missouri, Kansas, Nebraska, California, Oregon, and Washington. The are few county histories for South Dakota, North Dakota, Montana, Wyoming, New Mexico, Arizona, Utah, Nevada, and Idaho.

There are very few town histories for these states, Exceptions are Milwaukee, Kansas City, St. Louis, and Seattle.

In an effort to recommend at least one source for each state, the following are given:

### Wisconsin

*Wisconsin Magazine of History* (1917-present). Each volume includes an index.

## Minnesota

*Minnesota History* (1915 to the present). Each volume includes an index.

## Iowa

*Iowa Journal of History* (1903-60). There is an index for 1903-42, and each volume thereafter.
*Hawkeye Heritage* (1966-present). Each volume includes an index.

## Missouri

*Missouri Historical Review* (1906-present). There is an index for 1906-51 and each volume thereafter.
*Missouri Pioneers* (1967-76). Each volume includes an index.
*Missouri Miscellany* (a continuation of *Missouri Pioneers;* 1976-84). There is an index in each volume.
*Kansas City Genealogist* (1960 to the present). There is an index in each volume.

## Kansas

*Kansas Historical Quarterly* (1933-78). There is an index in each volume.
*Kansas History* (continuation of *Kansas Historical Quarterly;* 1978-present). Index in each volume.
*Treesearcher* (1959-present). There is an index in each volume.

## Oklahoma

*Oklahoma Genealogical Society Quarterly* (1972-77). There is an index in each volume.
*Tulsa Annals* (1966-80). There is an index in each volume.

## South Dakota

*South Dakota History* (1970-present). There is an index in each volume.
*Black Hills Nuggets* (1968-present). There is an index in each volume.

## North Dakota

*North Dakota Historical Quarterly* (1926-44). There is no index.

*North Dakota History* (1945-present). There is no index.
*Bismarck Mandan Historical and Genealogical Society* (1974-present). There is an index in each volume.

## Nebraska

*Nebraska History* (1922-present). There is an index in each volume.

## Nevada

*Nevada Historical Society Quarterly* (1957 to the present). There is no index.

## Wyoming

The Burton Collection holds only a few books on Wyoming. It does not have any historical or genealogical magazines for the state. The three most important items for genealogists are listed as follows: *Unita County: Its Place in History* by Elizabeth Arnold Stone, *Pioneer People of Douglas and Converse County, Wyoming* by Emma C. Adair, *Fort Bridger, Wyoming: A Brief History* by Robert S. Ellison.

## Montana

*Montana, the Magazine of Western History* (1951 to the present). There is no index.

## Colorado

*Colorado Magazine* (1923-80). There is no index.
*Colorado Heritage* (continuation of *Colorado Magazine*; 1981 to the present). There is no index.
*Colorado Genealogist* (1939-present). There is an index for 1939-48, and thereafter in each volume.

## New Mexico

*New Mexico Historical Review* (1926 to the present). There is an index in each volume.
*New Mexico Genealogist* (1962-76). There is an index in each volume.

## Arizona

*Journal of Arizona History* (1960 to the present). There is an index in each volume.

## Utah

*Utah Historical Quarterly* (1939-present). An index in each volume.
*Utah Genealogical and Historical Magazine* (1910-40). There is an index in each volume.
*Utah Genealogical Journal* (1972 to the present). There is no index.

## California

*California History* (1922 to the present). An index in each volume.
*The Searcher* (1963-78). There is no index.
*Ash Tree Echo* (1966 to the present). An index in each volume.
*Redwood Searcher* (1968-77). There is an index in each volume.

## Oregon

*Oregon Historical Quarterly* (1900 to the present). There is an index for 1900-1939 and in each volume thereafter.
*Bulletin of the Genealogical Forum of Portland, Oregon* (1951 to the present). There is an index in each volume.

## Idaho

*Idaho Yesterdays* (1957 to the present). An index in each volume.
*Idaho Genealogical Society Quarterly* (1958 to the present). There is no index.

## Washington

*Washington Historical Quarterly* (190635). An index in each volume.
*Pacific Northwest Quarterly* (continuation of *Washington Historical Quartery*; 1936 to the present). An index in each volume.
*Bulletin of the Seattle Genealogical Society* (1952 to the present). There is an index in each volume.

## Alaska and Hawaii

There are very few books in the Burton Collection on Alaska and Hawaii. The few on Alaska cover only the history of the state. The few on Hawaii also cover the history but include some works on the genealogy of the Hawaiian kings.

# 6
# Sources for Foreign Countries

## Canada

The Burton Collection's coverage of the majority of the Canadian provinces is rather general with the emphasis placed on Ontario and Quebec.

### Ontario

The histories of the Ontario counties are well represented in the Burton Collection. Various counties have published sets of papers or publications on their histories. These include Grimsby, Lennox and Addington, London and Middlesex, Kent, Niagara, and Waterloo counties.

*Families,* published by the Ontario Genealogical Society, is one of the best magazines for Ontario genealogical research. The Burton Collection has issues from its first publication in 1962 to the present. There is no index for this magazine.

Burton has a very good collection of atlases of Ontario counties. There is a plat, or drawing, for each township in the county, listing everyone who owned land in the township. The atlases were generally published in the late 1870s or 1880s and can be very helpful in locating a family between censuses. Unfortunately, these atlases are not indexed.

### Quebec

Since Detroit was founded by the French, the Burton Collection has always collected material on Quebec. One of the best sources for French-Canadian genealogy is *Dictionnaire Genealogique des Familles Canadiennes* by Cyprian Tanguay. Originally published in 1871-90, this seven-volume set was reprinted in 1969. It is in French but very easy to interpret. Individuals are listed alphabetically along with their birth, marriage death dates and their spouses. Children are listed with their birth dates also. A generational numbering system is used to allow the researcher to work back by generations. Frequently, references are made to a specific birthplace in France.

A correction and continuation of Tanguay is Rene Jette's *Diction-naire Genealogique des familles du Quebec, 1621-1730*. This work covers persons who were born in or came to Quebec prior to 1730. It includes baptisms, marriages, and deaths from 1621 to 1730. The work is arranged alphabetically by last name and chronologically by the date of marriage. For each line, the name is given, date and place of birth, baptism, marriage contract, marriage ceremony, death and burial, profession, date of immigration, and place of origin outside Quebec.

Doubtlessly, the most comprehensive work for French-Canadian genealogy is *Repertorie des Actes de Bateme, Mariage, Sepulture et des Rencensements du Quebec Ancien*. This thirty-volume work covers over 120 Roman Catholic parishes around Quebec City, Montreal, and Three Rivers from the early 1600s through 1749. It includes baptisms, marriages, burials, and censuses. It is arranged chronologically with the first seven volumes covering the 1600s and a separate alphabetical index in Volume 7. Volumes 8 through 17 cover the period 1700 to 1729 with an alphabetical index in Volumes 16 and 17. Volumes 18 through 30 cover 1730-49 with the index in Volumes 29 and 30. This set is without a doubt the most comprehensive work on early French-Canadian genealogy and should be checked thoroughly by any genealogist working on the Quebec area.

Another very good source for Quebec research are the marriage registers that have been transcribed by Rene Jette, Benoit Pontbriand and others. Burton's collection of these registers includes over 360 parishes. The registers are alphabetically arranged and give an individual's name, the parents' names including the mother's maiden name, the date of the marriage, and the spouse's name. Frequently, these registers cover years from the 1600s into the 1980s.

There is a good genealogical magazine for French-Canadian genealogy in the Burton Collection. The *Memoirs de la Societe Genealogique Canadiene-Francaise* first appeared in 1944, and the Burton Collection has a complete set of the magazine to the present. There is an index in each volume.

# England

The Burton Collection does not hold county or town histories for England. However, it does have an extensive set of parish registers covering the Anglican church. The records extend from the 1500s to the early 1800s. They are listed in the Vital Records Catalog No. 12. The registers are mostly marriages and visitations but also include baptisms, burials, and wills. Visitations were visits by representatives of the crown or heralds who fully recorded family names and pedigrees.

## Scotland

As with England, the Burton Collection does not have any histories of the counties of Scotland.

The best source for Scottish biography is Robert Chamber's *Lives of Illustrious and Distinguished Scottsmen . . . Scottish Biographical Dictionary*. This four-volume work, published in 1833, is arranged alphabetically and gives detailed information on early Scots.

The *Scottish Genealogist* is the best genealogical magazine for Scotland. Burton has all issues from the first in 1954 to the present. The early issues are indexed in each volume; the later ones are not.

## Ireland

The Burton Collection does not hold any county histories for Ireland, although it does have an excellent work on Irish genealogy. *Irish and Scotch Irish Ancestral Research* by Margaret Falley is a guide to genealogical records, methods, and sources in Ireland. Published in 1962, this two-volume work is the best on how-to-do Irish genealogy. Volume 1 lists repositories in Ireland and the types of records available there. Volume 2 discusses published records, unpublished family records, microfilm and where it is located, and suggests a bibliography for preliminary research in the United States.

Two genealogical magazines published on Irish genealogy are the *Irish Genealogist* and *Irish Ancestors*. Both publish source material on Ireland including family histories, vital records, and cemetery inscriptions. The Burton Collection holds issues of the *Irish Genealogist* for 1968 to the present. The issues of the *Irish Ancestors* extend from 1970 to the present. Both are indexed in each volume.

## The Caribbean

*Caribbeana* by Vere L. Oliver, published in 1910, is an excellent set on early Caribbean genealogy for the eighteenth and nineteenth centuries. This six-volume set, with an index in each volume, includes documents, genealogies, and charts.

# Bibliographical Index

The numbers in brackets following each entry refer to the page in the text upon which the reference may be found.

## Books and Other Sources

Adair, Emma C. *Pioneer People of Douglas and Converse County, Wyoming.* Douglas, Wyo.: 1962. (79)

*Archives of Maryland.* 72 vols. Baltimore: Maryland Historical Society, 1883-1972. (67)

Arnold, James N. *Vital Records of Rhode Island, 1636-1850.* 21 vols. Providence: Narragansett Historical Publications Co., 1891-1912. (63)

Austin, John Osborne. *Genealogical Dictionary of Rhode Island.* Albany: J. Munsell's and Sons, 1887. (63)

Baist, George W. *Baist's Real Estate Atlas of Surveys of Detroit Michigan.* Philadelphia: G. W. Baist, 1896-1955. (43)

Baldwin, Thomas. *Vital Records of Cambridge, Massachusetts to the Year 1850.* Boston: New England Historic and Genealogical Society, 1915. (48)

Barber, Gertrude A. *Deaths as listed in the New York Evening Post from Nov. 16, 1801-Oct. 15, 1835.* 12 vols. New York: New York Evening Post, 1933-37. (65)

Barber, Henry. *British Family Names.* 2nd ed. enlarged. London: E. Stock, 1903. Reprint, Detroit: Gale Research, 1968. (41)

Barbour, Lucius B. *Barbour Collection of Connecticut Vital Records Listed Alphabetically.* Under Individual Names, 81 reels. Under Names of Towns, 17 reels. Connecticut State Library. (64)

Belden, H. & Co. *Illustrated Historical Atlas of the County of Wayne, Michigan.* Chicago: H. Belden & Co., 1876. (9)

Black, George F. *Surnames of Scotland: Their Origin, Meaning and History.* New York: New York Public Library, 1946. (42)

*Blacks in Selected Newspapers, Censuses, and other Sources: An Index to Names and Subjects.* 2 vols. Boston: G. K. Hall, 1985. (47)

Blockson, Charles L. *Black Genealogy.* Englewood Cliffs, N.J.: Prentice-Hall, 1977. (47)

Burke, Sir John Bernard. *Encyclopedia of Heraldry.* 3rd ed. London: H. G. Bohn, 1851. (49)

_____. *Genealogical and Heraldic History of the Landed Gentry.* London: Burke's Peerage, 1836-38. (49)

_____. *The General Armory of England, Scotland, Ireland, and Wales.* London: Harrison & Sons, 1884. (49)

Burns, Annie Walker. *Indexes to Maryland Testamentary Proceedings.* 24 vols. Annapolis, Md.: The author, 1936-39. (67)

Carter, Clarence. *Territorial Papers of the United States.* 27 vols. Washington, D.C.: Government Printing Office, 1934-69. (74)

Canada. Public Archives, Manuscript Division. Population Schedules. Ottawa: Public Archives, 1842-91. (30)

*Census of the Slaves, 1755.* New York: N.p., 1850. (47)

Chadwick, Edward M. *Ontarian Families.* 2 vols. Toronto: Rolph, Smith & Co., 1895-98. (50)

Chambers, Robert. *Lives of Illustrious and Distinguished Scotsmen...Scottish Biographical Dictionary.* 4 vols. Glasgow: Blackie & Son, 1833-35. (83)

Clark, Peter H. *Black Brigade of Cincinnati: Being a Report of Its Labors and a Muster Roll of Its Members...* Cincinnati: Joseph B. Boyd, 1864. (48)

Colket, Meredith B. *Founders of Early American Families, Emigrants from Europe 1607-1657.* Cleveland: Order of Founders and Patriots, 1975. (41)

Connecticut Adjutant General's Office. *Record of Service of Men in the War of the Revolution, War of 1812, Mexican War.* Hartford: Connecticut Adjutant General's Office, 1889. (63)

Cotton, Jane Baldwin. *The Maryland Calendar of Wills.* 8 vols. Baltimore: W.J.C. Dulany, 1901-28. (67)

Daughters of the American Revolution. *DAR Patriot Index.* Washington, D.C.: 1966. (36, 40)

_____. *Lineage Books.* 166 vols. Washington, D.C.: DAR, 1896-1939. (40)

_____. *Library Catalog.* 2 vols. Washington, D.C.: DAR, 1982-1986. (24)

_____. Louisa St. Clair Chapter. *Birth Records from the Archives of Wayne County, Michigan.* 4 vols. Detroit: Michigan State Library and DAR Louisa St. Clair Chapter, 1936. (74)

_____. Louisa St. Clair Chapter. *Death Records of Elmwood Cemetery 1837-1870.* 4 vols. Detroit: DAR Louisa St. Clair Chapter, 1936. (74)

_____. Louisa St. Clair Chapter. *Death Records of Mount Elliott Cemetery.* 2 vols. Detroit: DAR Louisa St. Clair Chapter, 1937. (74)

_____. Louisa St. Clair Chapter. *Death Records of the Detroit Board of Health.* 5 vols. Detroit: DAR Louisa St. Clair Chapter, 1936. (74)

_____. Louisa St. Clair Chapter. *Early Land Transfers, Detroit and Wayne County, Michigan 1703- 1869.* 57 vols. Detroit: DAR Louisa St. Clair Chapter, 1939. (43, 75)

_____. Louisa St. Clair Chapter. *Marriage Records, from the Archives of Wayne County, Michigan 1835-1870.* 11 vols. Detroit: DAR Louisa St. Clair Chapter, 1936. (75)

_____. Louisa St. Clair Chapter. *Probate Records of Wayne County, Michigan.* 5 vols. Detroit: DAR Louisa St. Clair Chapter, 1936. (75)

_____. Louisa St. Clair Chapter. *Vital Records from the Detroit Free Press 1831-1868.* 17 vols. Detroit: DAR Louisa St. Clair, 1939. (74)

_____. Michigan. *DAR Bible and Pioneer Records.* 37 vols. DAR Michigan, 1921-61. (74)

Daughters of Founders and Patriots. *Lineage Books.* National Society of Daughters of Founders and Patriots. Washington, D. C. 37 volumes, 1910-84. (40)

Delaware Archives Commission. *Delaware Archives.* 5 vols. Wilmington: Mercantile Printing Co., 1911-16. (66)

Denissen, Christian. *Genealogy of French Families of the Detroit River Region 1701-1911.* Ed. Harold F. Powell. 2 vols. Detroit: Detroit Society for Genealogical Research, 1976. (76)

*Detroit City Directories* (73, 75)

*Detroit Telephone Directories* (73)

Dickson, Charles H. *1910 Annuity Roll of Ottawas and Chippewas in Michigan.* Washington, D.C.: National Archives and Records Service, 1972. (51)

*Dictionary Catalog of the Local History and Genealogy Division.* 18 vols. New York: Research Libraries of the New York Public Library, 1974. (22)

*Digested Summary of Alphabetical List of Private Claims which have been presented to the House of Representatives from the 1st to the 31st Congress.* 3 vols. Baltimore: Genealogical Publishing Co., 1970. (44)

*Documents Relating to the Colonial History of the State of New Jersey.* New Jersey Archives. First Series. 42 vols. Newark, N.J.: New Jersey Historical Society, 1880-1950. (66)

*Documents Relating to the Revolutionary History of the State of New Jersey.* New Jersey Archives. Second Series. 5 vols. Trenton: J.L. Murphy, 1901-17. (66)

Durant, Horace B. *The 1908 Census of the Chippewa Indians of Michigan.* Washington, D.C.: National Archives and Record Service, 1972. (51)

Eakle, Arlene, and Johni Cerny. *The Source: a Guidebook of American Genealogy.* Salt Lake City: Ancestry Publishing Co., 1984. (47)

Egle, William H. *Pennsylvania in the War of the Revolution: with Associated Battalions and Militia 1775-83.* 2 vols. Harrisburg: E.K. Meyers, 1896-98. (65)

Eichholz, Alice and James M. Rose. *Free Black Heads of Households in the New York Census, 1790-1830.* 5 vols. Detroit: Gale Research, 1981. (47)

Ellison, Robert S. *Fort Bridger, Wyoming: a Brief History.* Casper, Wyo.: Historical Landmark Commission of Wyoming, 1938. (79)

Falley, Margaret. *Irish and Scotch Irish Ancestral Research.* 2 vols. Evanston, Ill.: 1961-62. (83)

Farmer, John. *A Genealogical Register of the First Settlers of New England.* Reprinted with additions and corrections by Samuel G. Drake. Baltimore: Genealogical Publishing Co., 1976. (60)

_____. *Map of Wayne County, Michigan.* Detroit: John Farmer, 1855. (42)

Filby, P. William. *American and British Genealogy and Heraldry.* Chicago: American Library Association, 1970. (59)

_____. *Passenger and Immigration Lists Index.* 6 vols. Detroit: Gale Research, 1981-87. (31)

_____. *Philadelphia Naturalization Records.* Detroit: Gale Research, 1982. (65)

Fox-Davies, Arthur C. *Armorial Families.* 1st Tuttle ed. Rutland, Vt.: C. E. Tuttle Co., 1970. (49)

Giuseppi, Montague S., ed. *Naturalization of Foreign Protestants in America and the West Indian Colonies.* Baltimore: Genealogical Publishing Co., 1969. (65)

Glazier, Ira A. and Michael Tepper, eds. *The Famine Immigrants: Lists of Irish Immigrants Arriving at the Port of New York, 1846-51.* 6 vols. to date. Baltimore: Genealogical Pub. Co., 1984. (31)

*Goodspeed's History of the Counties of Tennessee.* Nashville: Goodspeed Publishing Co., 1886-87. (70)

Greenwood, Val D. *The Researchers Guide to American Genealogy.* Baltimore: Genealogical Publishing Co., 1974. (27)

Haller, Stephen E., and Robert Smith. *Register of Blacks in the Miami Valley: a Name Abstract 1804-57.* Dayton: Wright State University, 1977. (48)

*Hamburg Lists.* (33)

Hart, Henry. *City of Detroit, Michigan.* New York: Henry Hart, 1853. (10)

Hebert, Donald J. *Black Marriages in the Register of Blacks, St. Landry Church, Opelousas, Louisiana.* Vol. 3 of *Southwest Louisiana Records: Church and Civil Records 1831-1840.* Eunice, La.: The author, 1976. (48)

Hening, William. *The Statutes at Large; Being a Collection of all the Laws of Virginia from the First Session of the Legislature in the Year 1619.* 13 vols. Richmond: 1819-23. (68)

*Hereditary Register of the United States of America.* Washington, D.C.: United States Hereditary Register Inc., 1977. (41)

*Index to American Genealogies.* Albany: J. Munsell's and Sons, 1900. (21)

*International Genealogical Index (IGI).* Church of Jesus Christ of Latter-day Saints. (21)

Jacobus, Donald L. *Families of Ancient New Haven.* 8 vols. New Haven, Conn.: D.L. Jacobus, 1923-32. (64)

_____. History and Genealogy of the Families of Old Fairfield. 3 vols. in 12. New Haven, Conn.: Tuttle, Morehouse & Taylor, 1930-33. (64)

_____. *Index to Genealogical Periodicals.* 1932. Baltimore: Genealogical Publishing Co., 1978. (22)

Jette, Rene. *Dictionnaire Genealogique des Familles du Quebec 1621-1730.* Montreal: University of Montreal, 1983. (82)

Kaminkow, Marion J., ed. U.S. Library of Congress. *Genealogies in the Library of Congress.* 2 vols. Baltimore: Magna Carta Book Co., 1972. (23)

_____. U.S. Library of Congress. *Complement to the Genealogies in the Library of Congress.* Baltimore: Magna Carta Book Co., 1981. (23)

_____. U.S. Library of Congress. *United States Local Histories in the Library of Congress.* 5 vols. Baltimore: Magna Carta Book Co., 1975-76. (24)

Keller, Elizabeth. *Caldwell County, North Carolina Marriages, 1841-1866.* Baltimore: Gateway Press, 1982. (48)

Kelly, Patrick. *Irish Family Names.* Chicago: O'Connor and Kelly, 1939. (42)

Konarski, Szyman. *Armorial de la Noblesses Polonaise Titree.* Paris: Marcel Orbec, 1958. (49)

Loomis, Frances, comp. *Michigan Biography Index.* 11 vols. Detroit: Detroit Public Library, 1954. (73)

Lorenz-Meyer, Eduard. *Hamburgische Wappenrolle.* Hamburg: C.A. Starke, 1912. (49)

McAuslan, William A. *Mayflower Index.* 3 vols. Revised by Lewis E. Neff. Boston: General Society of Mayflower Descendants, 1960. (62)

McLysaght, Edward. *Surnames of Ireland.* Shannon: Irish University Press, 1969. (42)

Manarin, Louis H. *North Carolina Troops, 1861-1865.* 8 vols. to date. Raleigh: State Dept. of Archives and History, 1966-. (68)

Mansfield, John B. *History of the Great Lakes.* 2 vols. Chicago: J. H. Beers & Co., 1899. (71)

Massachusetts. Secretary of the Commonwealth. *Massachusetts Soldiers and Sailors of the Revolutionary War.* 27 vols. Boston: Wright & Potter, 1896-1908. (62)

*Mayflower Families Through Five Generations.* 3 vols. to date. Plymouth: General Society of Mayflower Descendants, 1975-80. (63)

Michigan Adjutant General's Office. *First Michigan Colored Infantry.* Vol. 46 of *Record of Service of Michigan Volunteers in the Civil War 1861-1865.* Kalamazoo: Ihling Bros. and Everhard, 1900-. (48)

_____. *Record of Service of Michigan Volunteers in the Civil War 1861-1865.* 46 vols. Kalamazoo: Ihling Bros. & Everhard, 1900-. (73)

Michigan. State Department of Public Health. *Index of Death Records 1867-1914.* 13 reels. (60, 74)

Michigan. State Department of Public Health. *Index of Marriage Records, 1872-1921.* 21 reels. (60, 74)

Mills, Elizabeth S. *Natichitoches, 1800-1821.* Translated Abstracts of Register #5 of St. Francis des Natichitoches, Louisiana. Vol. 4 of *Cane River Creole Series.* New Orleans: Polyanthos, Inc., 1980. (48)

National Genealogical Society. *Index of Revolutionary War Pension Applications.* Washington, D.C.: National Genealogical Society, 1966. (36)

New England Historic Genealogical Society. *Greenlaw Index of the New England Historic Genealogical Society.* 2 vols. Boston: G. K. Hall, 1979. (22)

New Hampshire. *The Provincial Papers, Documents and Records Relating to the Province of New Hampshire.* 40 vols. Concord: George E. Jenks, 1867-1943. (61)

Newberry Library, Chicago. *Genealogical Index of the Newberry Library.* 4 vols. Boston: G. K. Hall, 1960. (22)

Newman, Debra L. *List of Free Black Heads of Families in the First Census of the United States, 1790.* Washington, D.C.: National Archives and Record Service, 1973. (47)

Niescecki, Kaspar. *Herbarz Polski Kaspara Niesieckiego.* 10 vols. Lipsku: Breitkopf: Haertel, 1839-46. (50)

Oliver, Vere L., ed. *Caribbeana.* 6 vols. London: Mitchell, Hughes, and Clarke, 1909-10. (83)

Order of the Founders and Patriots of America. *Registers.* 5 Vols. New York: Order of the Founders and Patriots of America, 1902-80. (41)

Ostrowski, Juliusz R. *Ksiega Herbowa Radow Polskich.* Warszawa: Gebethner Wolff, 1900-06. (50)

*Parish and Vital Records Listings.* Church of Jesus Christ of Latter-day Saints. (23)

*Pennsylvania Archives.* 122 vols. Philadelphia: Joseph Severns & Co., 1852-1935. (65)

Pennsylvania German Society. *Proceedings and Addresses.* 53 vols. Lancaster, Pa.: Pennsylvania German Society, 1891-1948. (65)

_____. *Publications.* 10 vols. Lancaster, Pa.: Pennsylvania German Society, 1953-66. (65)

Polk, R. L. and Company. *Marine Directory of the Great Lakes.* Detroit: R. L. Polk, 1888. (71)

Providence. City Registrar. *Alphabetical Index of the Births, Marriages, and Deaths Recorded in Providence.* 25 vols. Providence: S. S. Rider, 1879-1936. (63)

Rankin, Lois. "Detroit Nationality Groups." *Michigan History Magazine,* 23 (1939), 129-205. (46)

*Rasher's Map of Detroit, Michigan.* 3 vols. Chicago: Rasher Map Publishing Co., 1888. (43)

*Records of the Town of Plymouth 1636-1783.* 3 vols. Plymouth: Avery and Doten, 1889-1903. (63)

*Registre de la Paroisse de l' Assumption. Aug. 31, 1752 - Dec. 31, 1824.* Copyist Jacques Hercklar. 3 vols. Detroit: N.p., 1890.

*Registre des Paroisses Exterieures 1810-1833.* Copyist Jacques Hercklar. Detroit: N.p., 1890. (77)

*Registre de St. Anne. 1704-1848.* Copyist Jacques Hercklar. 5 vols. in 7. Detroit: N.p., 1890. (76)

Reid, William D. *The Loyalists in Ontario.* Lambertville, N.J.: Hunterdon House, 1973. (50)

Reitstap, Johannes B. *Armorial General.* 6 vols. LeHaye: M. Nijhoff. 1926-1950. (49)

*Repertoire des Actes de Bateme, Mariage, Sepulture et des Rencensements du Quebec Ancien.* 30 vols. Montreal: University of Montreal, 1980. (82)

Rider, Fremont. *American Genealogical-Biographical Index to American Genealogical, Biographical, and Local History Materials.* 151 vols. to date. Middletown, Conn.: Godfrey Memorial Library, 1952- . (21)

Robbins, Charles D. *Record of Marriages of Henry County, Tennessee, 1881-1900.* 2 vols. Paris, Tenn: Robbins & Walker, 1983. (48)

Robinson, Eugene. *Atlas of the City of Detroit and Suburbs.* Detroit: Eugene Robinson, 1885. (43)

Rogers, Ellen S., ed. *Genealogical Periodical Annual Index.* 25 vols. to date. Bladensburg, Md.: Genealogical Recorders, 1962-. (22)

Russell, Donna Valley. *Michigan Censuses 1710-1830.* Detroit: Detroit Society of Genealogical Research, 1982. (30)

Savage, James. *Genealogical Dictionary of the First Settlers of New England.* 4 vols. Boston: Little, Brown & Co., 1860-62. (60)

Scharf, Thomas J. *History of Delaware 1609-1888.* 2 vols. Philadelphia: L. J. Richards & Co., 1888. Index. Gladys M. Coghlan & Dale Fields. 3 vols. Wilmington: Historical Society of Delaware, 1976. (66)

Smith, Clifford Neal. *Federal Land Series.* 4 vols. Chicago: American Library Association, 1972. (44)

Smith, Elsdon. *Dictionary of American Family Names.* New York: Harper, 1956. (41)

Spear, Dorothea N. *Bibliography of American Directories through 1860.* Worcester, Mass.: American Antiquarian Society, 1961. (38)

Spradling, Mary M. *In Black and White: A Guide to Magazine Articles, Newspaper Articles and Books, Concerning more than 15,000 Black Individuals and Groups.* Detroit: Gale Research, 1980. (47)

Sprenger, Bernice Cox. *Guide to the Manuscripts in the Burton Historical Collection, Detroit Public Library.* Detroit: Burton Historical Collection, 1985. (53)

State Historical Society of Wisconsin. *Collections.* 31 vols. Madison: State Historical Society of Wisconsin, 1855-1931. (76)

Stone, Elizabeth Arnold. *Unita County: Its Place in History.* Laramie, Wyo.: The Laramie Printing Company, 1924. (79)

Strohl, Hugo. *Deutsche Wappenrolle.* (49)

Strassburger, R. and William J. Hinke, eds. *Pennsylvania German Pioneers 1727-1809. 3 vols.* Norristown, Penn.: Pennsylvania German Society, 1934.

Stryker-Rodda, Kenn. *Genealogical Research: Methods and Sources.* 2 vols. Washington, D.C.: American Society of Genealogists, 1983. (47)

Swem, Earl G. *Virginia Historical Index.* 2 vols. Roanoke, Va.: Stone Printing & Manufacturing Co., 1934-36. (68)

Tanguay, Cyprian. *Dictionnaire Genealogique des Familles Canadiennes.* 7 vols. Montreal: E. Senecal & Fils, 1871-90. (81)

Tennessee Civil War Centennial Commission. *Tennesseans in the Civil War.* 2 parts. Nashville: Tennessee Civil War Centennial Commission, 1964-65. (70)

United Empire Loyalist Centennial Committee. *Centennial of the Settlement of Upper Canada by the United Empire Loyalists 1784-1884.* Toronto: Rose Pub. Co., 1885. (50)

U.S. Census Office. *Population Schedules, 1790-1910.* Washington, D.C.: National Archives. (26, 27)

U.S. Congress. *American State Papers.* 38 vols. Washington, D.C.: Gales and Seaton, 1832-61. (43)

U.S. National Archives. *Passenger Lists of Vessels Arriving at New York.* 371 reels. Washington, D. C.: National Archives. (31)

_____. *Revolutionary War Pension and Bounty Land Warrant Application Files.* 2,670 reels. (36)

U.S. National Archives and Records Service. *Index of Compiled Service Records of Volunteer Union Soldiers Who Served with U.S. Colored Troops.* Washington, D.C.: National Archives Trust Fund Board, 1979. (48)

_____. *Slave Schedules 1850 and 1860.* Washington, D.C.: National Archives Trust Fund Board, 1985. (47)

U.S. Pension Bureau. *List of Pensioners on the Roll January 1, 1883....* 5 vols. Washington, D.C.: Government Printing Office, 1883. (47)

Vermont. *The Rolls of the Soldiers in the Revolutionary War 1775-1783.* Rutland, Vt.: The Tuttle Co., 1904. (61)

Virginia. *Calendar of Virginia State Papers and other Manuscripts.* 11 vols. Richmond: the State of Virginia, 1875-93. (68)

Wayne State University. Department of Sociology and Anthropology. *Ethnic Groups in Detroit: 1951.* Detroit: Wayne State University, 1951. (45)

Walker, Frank. *Winston County, Alabama Marriages, 1891-1900.* Cullman, Ala.: Gregath Co., 1980. (48)

Walker, James D. *Black Genealogy: How to Begin.* Athens, Ga.: University of Georgia, Center for Continuing Education, 1977. (47)

Ward, Margaret. *Genealogical Sources for Afro-American Family Research in the Burton Historical Collection and the Detroit Public Library.* Detroit: Burton Historical Collection, 1985. (46)
West Virginia. Auditor's Office. *SIMS Index to Land Grants in West Virginia.* Charleston, W.Va.: West Virginia Auditor's Office, 1952 (67)
Woodson, Carter G. *Free Negro Heads of Families in the United States in 1830...* Washington, D.C.: The Association for the Study of Negro Life and History, 1925. (47)

# Magazines

*Alabama Genealogical Register* (69)
*The American Genealogist* (8, 25, 64)
*American Heritage* (24)
*Americana* (25)
*Arkansas Family Historian* (70)
*Ash Tree Echo* (80)
*Bismarck Mandan Historical and Genealogical Society, Publications* (79)
*Black Hills Nuggets* (78)
*Bulletin of the Genealogical Forum of Portland, Oregon* (80)
*Bulletin of the Seattle Genealogical Society* (80)
*Calendar of Virginia State Papers* (68)
*California History* (80)
*Central Texas Genealogical Society Quarterly* (70)
*Colorado Genealogist* (79)
*Colorado Heritage* (79)
*Colorado Magazine* (79)
*Daughters of the American Revolution Magazine* (25)
*Detroit Historical Society Bulletin* (24)
*Detroit Society for Genealogical Research Magazine* (8, 24, 29, 30, 76)
*Essex Institute Historical Collections* (22, 62)
*Families* (81)
*Filson Club History Quarterly* (70)
*Flint Genealogical Quarterly* (72)
*Florida Genealogist* (69)
*Genealogical Helper* (8, 25)
*Genealogical Magazine of New Jersey* (66)
*Georgia Genealogical Magazine* (69)
*Hawkeye Heritage* (78)
*Heart of Texas Records* (70)
*Hoosier Genealogist* (72)

*Oklahoma Genealogical Society Quarterly* (78)
*Old Northwest Genealogical Quarterly* (71)
*Oregon Historical Quarterly* (80)
*Pacific Northwest Quarterly* (80)
*Records of the Columbia Historical Society* (67)
*Redwood Searcher* (80)
*Register of the Kentucky State Historical Society* (70)
*Scottish Genealogist* (83)
*The Searcher* (80)
*South Carolina Historical and Genealogical Magazine* (69)
*South Carolina Historical Magazine* (69)
*South Dakota History* (78)
*Stirpes* (69)
*Telescope* (71)
*Tree Talks* (8, 65)
*Treesearcher* (78)
*Tulsa Annals* (78)
*Tyler's Quarterly* (68)
*Utah Genealogical and Historical Magazine* (80)
*Utah Genealogical Journal* (80)
*Utah Historical Quarterly* (80)
*Virginia Genealogist* (68)
*Virginia Historical Register* (68)
*Virginia Magazine* (68)
*Washington Historical Quarterly* (80)
*Western Maryland Genealogy* (66)
*William and Mary Quarterly* (68)
*Wisconsin Magazine of History* (77)

# Newspapers

*Ann Arbor News* (8)
*Boston Transcript* (21)
*Cheboygan Democrat* (73)
*Columbian Centinel and Massachusetts Federalist* (44)
*Democratic Free Press and Michigan Intelligencer* (13)
*Der Arme Teufel* (73)
*Detroit Daily Advertiser* (45)
*Detroit Free Press* (8, 13, 45, 73)
*Detroit Gazette* (45)
*Detroit Journal* (45)

*Detroit News* (45, 73)
*Lansing Journal* (73)
*London Chronicle* (44)
*Michigan Essay or Impartial Observer* (13, 44)
*Michigan Volksblatt* (8)
*National Intelligencer* (44)
*New York Herald* (44)
*Pennsylvania Gazette* (44)
*Pontiac Daily Press* (73)
*Pontiac Gazette* (8, 44)
*Sanilac Jeffersonian* (44, 73)
*Voice of the Fugitive* (44)

# Manuscripts

Bethel A.M.E. Church, Detroit. Parish Register of Trustee Board Minutes, Baptismal, Marriage and Membership Registers, 1911-69. 1 reel. (48)

Campbell Chapel A.M.E. Church. Marriage Register, November 4, 1896-December 10, 1924. Chatham, Ontario: 1 reel. (48)

Central Methodist Church, 1820-1970. (55)

Childrens' Aid Society, 1860-1942. (55)

Childrens' Home of Detroit Papers, 1836-1969. (55)

Christ Church, 1846-1906. (55)

Congregation Beth El, 1850-1969. (55)

Malcolm Dade, 1831-1976. (56)

Detroit House of Correction, 1861-1983. (58)

Detroit Notarial Records, 1737-95. (58)

Richard R. Elliott Papers. Passage Register. 1851-69. (35)

Detroit Records Court. Naturalization Papers 1852-1906. (33, 35)

First Parish Church, Brookfield, Massachusetts, 1817-57. (56)

First Presbyterian Church, 1833-1963. (55)

Fort Street Presbyterian Church, 1849-1962. (55)

Grace Episcopal Church, Mt. Clemens, Michigan, 1868-1966. (56)

Grosse Pointe Memorial Church, 1860-1973. (55)

Stephen Hull Papers, 1800-12. (53)

Charles I. Kanter Papers, 1868-85. (53)

Montreal Notarial Records, 1682-1822. (58)

George Moore Papers, 1788-1810. (53)

New England Society of Detroit, 1895-1916. (55)

Northcross Family, 1899-1973. (56)

Papers of the Sons of the American Revolution, Michigan Chapter, 1890-1973 (55)

Pelham Family, 1851-1948. (56)

Redford Methodist Episcopal Church, 1873-1924. (55)

Riverside Lutheran Church, 1907-65. (55)

St. John's Church, Sandwich, Ontario, 1807-57. (56)

St. Joseph, Michigan, Catholic Mission, 1720-72. (56)

St. Matthew's and St. Joseph's Episcopal Church. Parish Registers, 1894-1975. 1 reel. (48)

St. Paul's Cathedral, 1820-1908. (55)

Second Baptist Church. Parish Register, 1935-79. 2 reels. (48)

Society of Colonial Wars, Michigan, 1899-1944. (55)

Society of Mayflower Descendants, Detroit Chapter, 1901-43. (55)

Sons of the American Revolution, Michigan Chapter, 1890-1973. (55)

Tabernacle Baptist Church, 1859-65. (55)

Trumbull Avenue Presbyterian Church, 1883-1924. (55)

United States General Hospital, 1864-65. (56)

Wayne County Marriage Returns, 1818-88. (56)

Wayne County Register of Deeds. Tax Assessment Rolls, 1839-73. (56)

Woodmere Cemetery, 1871-1913. (56)

# Index